A Bias for Action

Also by Sumantra Ghoshal:

Managing Across Borders: The Transnational Solution
(with Christopher A. Bartlett).
Harvard Business School Publishing, 2002.

*The Individualized Corporation: A Fundamentally
New Approach to Management*
(with Christopher A. Bartlett).
HarperCollins Publishers, 1999.

*The Differentiated Network: Organizing Multinational
Corporations for Value Creation*
(with Nitin Nohria).
Jossey-Bass, 1997.

Transnational Management: Text, Cases and Readings
(with Christopher A. Bartlett and Julian Birkinshaw).
Richard D. Irwin, 2003.

Managing Radical Change
(with Gita Piramal and Christopher A. Bartlett).
Penguin Books, 2000.

The Strategy Process: Concepts, Contexts and Cases
(with Henry Mintzberg, Joseph Lampel,
and James Brian Quinn).
Pearson Education, 2003.

Organization Theory and the Multinational Corporation
(coedited with Eleanor Westney).
MacMillan, 1993.

THOMAS WOLFE

by B. R. McELDERRY, Jr.
University of Southern California

 TUSAS 50

Twayne Publishers, Inc.   ::   New York

Library of Congress Catalog Card Number: 63-20609

MANUFACTURED IN THE UNITED STATES OF AMERICA BY
UNITED PRINTING SERVICES, INC.
NEW HAVEN, CONN.

731663

FOR FRANCES

ABOUT THE AUTHOR

BRUCE R. McELDERRY, Jr., has been Professor of English at the University of Southern California since 1950. A graduate of Grinnell College, Professor McElderry took his Ph.D. at the University of Iowa in 1925. Before coming to the University of Southern California in 1946, he taught at the University of Wisconsin, Western Reserve University, and the State College of Washington. He has been visiting professor at New York University and the University of North Carolina.

Professor McElderry has edited Hamlin Garland's *Main-Travelled Roads* and *Boy Life on the Prairie*; A. B. Longstreet's *Georgia Scenes*; Owen Chase's *A Narrative of the Whale-Ship Essex* (a major source for Melville's *Moby Dick*); and *Mark Twain's Contributions to the Galaxy, 1868-1871*. He has also contributed to various professional journals.

Professor McElderry is a member of Phi Beta Kappa, the Modern Language Association, the American Studies Association, the Philological Association of the Pacific Coast, and the American Association of University Professors. In 1960 he was chairman of the University of Southern California Senate.

A Bias for Action

*How Effective Managers Harness
Their Willpower, Achieve Results,
and Stop Wasting Time*

Heike Bruch
Sumantra Ghoshal

HARVARD BUSINESS SCHOOL PRESS
Boston, Massachusetts

Library of Congress Cataloging-in-Publication Data
Bruch, Heike.
    A bias for action : how effective managers harness their willpower, achieve results, and stop wasting time / Heike Bruch, Sumantra Ghoshal.
        p. cm.
Includes bibliographical references and index.
    ISBN 1-59139-408-2
  1. Management. I. Ghoshal, Sumantra. II. Title.
    HD31.B76836 2004
    658.4—dc22

                                                              2003025724

16867

To our families with love

CONTENTS

PREFACE

I N HUMAN LIFE, some aspects are context specific; they arise
at a particular time and place, as a unique event, practice, or
challenge. Others, however, are enduring, forever the same. This
book embraces one challenge in human existence that was, is, and
always will be—the challenge of taking purposeful, persistent
action to achieve a goal.

About two millennia ago, Lucius Annaeus Seneca—the states-
man and philosopher whom Caligula exiled and Nero forced to
commit suicide—wrote:

> We must cut down on all this dashing about that a great many
> people indulge in, as they throng about houses and theatres and
> fora: they intrude into other people's affairs, always giving the
> impression of being busy. If you ask one of them as he comes out
> of a house, "Where are you going? What do you have in mind?"
> he will reply, "I really don't know; but I'll see some people, I'll do
> something." They wander around aimlessly looking for employ-
> ment, and they do not what they intended but what they hap-
> pened to run across. Their roaming is idle and pointless, like ants
> crawling over bushes, which purposelessly make their way right
> up to the topmost branch and then all the way down again. Many
> people live a life like these creatures, and you could not unjustly
> call it busy idleness.[1]

This book confronts busy idleness. We write about managers, because management is our area of professional work and it is in the context of managerial work that we have studied this aspect of human behavior, but the issue is by no means limited to that context. Busy idleness is a disease that affects everybody and pervades every aspect of life—academics fall victim to it just as much as managers, and all of us fall victim to it in our personal lives just as much as in our professional lives. *Active nonaction*, our term for busy idleness, prevents us not just from achieving tranquility of mind, which was Seneca's concern, but from making the most of our lives, of ourselves.

"So let all your activity be directed to some object, let it have some end in view," wrote Seneca. In this book, we repeat that relatively obvious yet profoundly important advice. We believe that people can take purposeful action, and we have witnessed that behavior. Clearly, no one can act purposefully all the time, in all that one does. We must occasionally pause and smell the roses. But we can act purposefully some of the time, in some of what we do. In those times and through those actions, often when we least expect it, we discover purpose in life itself. Each one of us can make a difference, not just in our own circumstances but also in the state and direction of our family, our community, our corporation, and our world—only by engaging in purposeful action.

Enough about the content of the book; if the belief behind the book interests you, do read on to learn why and how people like you can take purposeful action and then help others do the same. Enduring problems, alas, never have definite solutions. One can only chip away at them, and ours is another attempt to chip away at the same issue that Seneca pondered over in A.D. 60. While we lack Seneca's clarity of thinking and marvelous prose, we do share one quality with him: We have tried to provide as practical and down-to-earth advice as he did. We hope that every reader of this book, whether a CEO or a frontline manager—indeed a doctor, an artist, a student, a teacher, a gardener, a priest, a public servant, a parent, or someone engaged in any other profession or pursuit—will find at least one or two ideas here that will help him or her develop a bias for action a little more frequently and more effectively than before.

No one can write a book without many others helping in significant ways. Of all those who helped us, one individual stands out simply because without his contribution the journey of research that led to this book would have taken a completely different route—Thomas Sattelberger. He supported us throughout the entire process, not only in the research that we conducted in his company, Lufthansa, but also when we struggled to shape our ideas and interpretations. We would like to give him our utmost thanks.

The other person who played a similarly invaluable role was Sharon Wilson, the assistant to one of us but a friend to both. She smoothed the process from the background—not only the logistics of researching and writing but also the interactions between two highly strung colleagues.

We are deeply indebted to all the companies and all the managers who participated in the study, giving us generously not only their time but also their knowledge and perspectives. We mention a few of them in the book, but many others who taught us a lot go unnamed. Sometimes we can study ants, or pigeons, and write about people. But when human imagination and will are the phenomena of interest, only observation of human behavior can yield insights. Without a large number of people allowing us to study their behaviors, and some of them helping us interpret and abstract from those behaviors, we could not have developed the understanding of action-taking and willpower—albeit small and limited—that we have developed. We sincerely thank all of them and hope that the book will assure them that they spent their time well with us.

London Business School (LBS), where one of us has his permanent intellectual home and the other built a temporary abode, has supported our work immensely. In this book, we describe the sirens of organizational life—the continuous stream of distractions and "noise" that, in most organizations, diffuse people's attention and prevent them from engaging in purposeful action. LBS kept all the distractions away, allowing us to focus on our research and writing. University of St. Gallen similarly deserves our thanks for proving such a wonderful place to think and work, and for providing an exceptionally energizing environment.

We are also grateful to the Advanced Institute of Management Research (AIM) in the United Kingdom, which provided a generous fellowship to the second author and also a community of colleagues whose help and advice improved the quality of our thinking and analysis.

As academics, we never write five words where fifty will do. Lucy McCauley helped us transform this manuscript in the process of publishing, both by making the ideas and the arguments simpler and sharper, and by translating the language from German English and Indian English into just English. Kirsten Sandberg, our editor at Harvard Business School Press, has long been also a personal friend. She led us through the entire publishing process with firmness and ease and helped us significantly improve the quality and accessibility of the manuscript. We owe a lot to both Lucy and Kirsten, and to their colleagues at Harvard Business School Publishing who worked behind the scenes to shape this book into its present form.

—*Heike Bruch, St. Gallen, Switzerland*
Sumantra Ghoshal, London

Part One

Harnessing Your Willpower to Achieve Results

ONE

Management Is the Art of Doing and Getting Done

THINK BACK over the past three years. Have you ever spotted a chance to do something valuable for your company—a project that would really shake things up—but for whatever reason, you did not pursue it? Perhaps you just could not get started, or maybe you did begin the project but then gave up when you hit the first big roadblock.

If this has happened to you, you are by no means an exception. In fact, in our research we have found that such inaction is indeed the rule. Despite all their knowledge and competence, despite their influence and the resources they have at their disposal, most managers spend their time making the inevitable happen—instead of putting their energy into those exceptional things that create a company's future. Beyond their routine day-to-day tasks, most managers simply do not grab opportunities to achieve something significant.

Why? These executives usually offer "good reasons"—a nay-saying boss or a tight budget. But that is rarely the whole story. Rather, the reason most managers fail lies within the managers themselves. Consider the following case.[1]

Laura McCormick's Story

Laura McCormick had just landed the most challenging role of her career.[2] IBG, a $7 billion conglomerate, had acquired her employer, Delta Technologies, a telecommunications supplier—and appointed her, at thirty-three, one of two instructors in IBG's much-touted total quality program. Who better than McCormick to do the job? Energetic, enthusiastic, and articulate, she had risen quickly in her seven years at Delta. Tim Dermott, her boss and mentor as well as Delta's vice president of engineering, valued McCormick enough to nominate her for this highly visible position.

Dermott had ulterior motives. His relationship with Alan Sartora, Delta's vice president of operations and newly appointed head of the total quality program, reflected a long-standing divide between Delta engineering and operations. Their managerial styles differed as well; Sartora deemed Dermott "too soft and undemanding" of his people and not sensitive enough to Delta's cost pressures. Sartora valued fire-fighting types like Sam Butler, a manager from the factory floor, whom he installed as the other instructor.

Now leading the total quality project, Sartora was clearly positioning himself for Delta's CEO role. Having sought the total quality appointment himself, Dermott wanted someone on the project who could do the job without undoing their relationship. McCormick fit the bill.

Early in her new position, however, McCormick began to stall. Having squabbled with Sam Butler before, she considered him entirely unsuitable for teaching and avoided him whenever possible. Despite the uninspiring three-week instructor training session, their first program teaching together went well: Mc-Cormick liked the instruction materials, and she found the participants enthusiastic, voicing a range of ideas for improving the company.

She quickly discovered that, while the program encouraged employee empowerment, senior managers usually ignored or stigmatized workers who asked for changes. Even a straightforward improvement project that she considered a quick win for the total quality program got stuck. Despite McCormick's constant pushing, nothing happened for more than four months. "By the time we solved the problem, the bureaucratic hurdles had killed the enthusiasm, and we had nothing to celebrate," she said. A series of such incidents left McCormick doubting whether any of the company's senior managers, including Sartora, really wanted change.

In the midst of these doubts, Delta's president, Dave Croft—with whom Dermott and McCormick had been closely aligned—retired, and IBG announced that Sartora would replace him. Sartora further consolidated his power by dividing engineering in two, giving Dermott the smaller piece—in effect, demoting Dermott.

Still, for three months McCormick pushed on, running one program after another, attending meetings, tackling problems that cropped up, and spending hours each day answering e-mails and returning phone calls. She felt that she was constantly busy, working overtime for total quality, yet there were no clear big wins for the project. Instead, three rounds of layoffs ensued, each more severe than the last. Employee morale was dipping, and Delta was heading for its first quarterly loss. "I was lying to employees, creating false hopes, and raising expectations," McCormick said, "all while the organization was actually going in the opposite direction."

When McCormick finally asked to relinquish the teaching role, Sartora responded, "People *like* you. You have credibility, and you are good. I do not want to lose you." But she had already read the writing on the wall. Dermott was powerless; Croft was gone; senior management was noncommittal. McCormick polished her résumé and resigned a month later.

How does a competent, high-potential manager like McCormick end up failing at such an important assignment? What, exactly, kept her from making total quality a real success?

The Truth About "Busy" Managers

Laura McCormick's story is in no way special. Everyone has probably experienced or witnessed hundreds, maybe thousands, of such instances in companies around the world. We have all been in a situation where, no matter what we tried, bureaucracy and budget constraints stifled our efforts at change. We have all seen how political one-upmanship can often take precedence over creating real, lasting improvement. No doubt, the conflict between Alan Sartora and Tim Dermott politicized the environment. Clearly, the organizational systems and processes were not ready for total quality, especially when senior management was not pushing for change. Total quality was the rhetoric; McCormick was caught between the rhetoric and the organizational reality.

But is that the full story? What could have happened, for example, if instead of avoiding contact with Sam Butler, Laura had tried to build a great relationship with him from the beginning? He was in Sartora's good books. Perhaps the two of them could have begun to bridge the gap between Sartora and Dermott. But more to the point, although McCormick kept very busy running programs, she did not appear to spend much time really thinking about the total quality project overall, or developing a clear vision of what she wanted it to look like. In fact, she seemed surprised when problems surfaced. What if, instead of gradually withdrawing her energy from the project, she had anticipated problems and possible solutions? Rather than blaming management, what would have happened had she asked herself about her own role in the project's failures?

McCormick was not passive, stupid, or lazy. On the contrary, her days—like most managers'—were a constant stream of meetings, conference calls, e-mails, voice mails, pages, and so on, with no time to think.

That is precisely the problem. By its very nature, a manager's job leaves little room for reflection. The result? Contrary to what we might hope to hear, managers tend to ignore or postpone dealing with the organization's most crucial issues. After all, those problems usually require a big-picture perspective—which means reflection, systematic planning, creative thinking, and above all, time. Instead, operational activities requiring more immediate attention squeeze important problems out. Daily routines, superficial behaviors, poorly prioritized or unfocused tasks leech managers' capacities—making unproductive busyness perhaps the most critical behavioral problem in large companies.

How does this happen? How do smart, talented executives end up losing valuable time and energy, rather than acting in truly productive ways? Situational factors rarely account entirely for this lack of purposeful, goal-directed action-taking. In fact, as a rule, managers' jobs provide sufficient scope and freedom to act— as McCormick's position clearly did. Yet relatively few managers are aware that they are free to take action, and of those who are, few deliberately exploit their action-taking opportunities. Instead, they get lost in the stream of their own activities and spend their time making the inevitable happen—rather than actively making happen what really could achieve results.

The problem for these executives, then, is not a lack of knowledge or even resources. McCormick, for example, had all the training she needed to make total quality work—and Sartora made it clear to her that he was behind her all the way. The real problem is that even though McCormick and executives like her *know* what to do, they simply do not *do* those things. Instead they spend their time spinning their wheels, as McCormick did, attending meetings and responding to every little query and problem—anything but accomplishing the mission with which they were charged in the first place.

Yet their success as managers depends on meeting their goals. "Management was, is, and always will be the same thing: the art of getting things done," write Bob Eccles and Nitin Nohria, both professors at Harvard Business School, in their celebrated book *Beyond the Hype*.[3] "And to get things done, managers must act themselves and mobilize collective action on the part of others." The gap between knowledge and action, however, stretches wide—and few managers seem able to cross it.

None of this is news, of course. We are not the first to identify the kind of behavior that McCormick exhibited—*active nonaction*, as we call it—as a managerial hazard. Researchers such as Stanford's Jeffrey Pfeffer and Robert Sutton have studied it. Lamenting what they describe as the pervasive corporate "knowing-doing gap," Pfeffer and Sutton ask, "Why do so much education and training, management consulting, and business research and so many books and articles produce so little change in what managers and organizations actually do? . . . Why [does] knowledge of what needs to be done frequently fail to result in action or behavior consistent with that knowledge?"[4] Managers, too, have long complained about the problem of active nonaction but have not fully understood the underlying dynamics.

What can managers like McCormick do to become more purposeful in their work? How can senior leaders like Sartora shape organizations in which they—and others—feel freer to take action? This book will examine the hows and whys of active nonaction, based on our ten-year research into the behavior of busy managers at nearly a dozen large companies. (See the appendix, "How We Studied Willpower" for details of our research.) More important, it will show leaders how to improve not only their own effectiveness but also that of their managers—and help everyone in the organization move toward more consistently purposeful action.

The Promise of Purposeful Action

What do we mean, exactly, by *purposeful action*? Consistent, conscious, and energetic behavior that shows "a bias for action." That is the title of this book, and it is the one attribute of companies that Tom Peters and Robert Waterman identify as underpinning all other criteria of excellence.[5] Yet, at the same time, purposeful action is very different from Peters and Waterman's "ready, fire, aim" prescription for building a bias for action. Experimentation; make a little, sell a little; remaining flexible to disengage quickly—that is what they saw as the essence of action-taking in companies.

While experimentation and flexibility are important for companies, in our observation the most critical challenge for companies is exactly the opposite: determined, persistent, and relentless action-taking to achieve a purpose, against all odds. Driven by deep personal commitment to the goal that cuts out distractions and overcomes difficulties, purposeful action is not a quick shuffle or mere flirtation with ideas. It is not the superficial attempt to achieve something. It is action-taking to produce certain results, with undivided resolve. Although external issues in an organization can make this kind of action-taking especially difficult—as they clearly did in Laura McCormick's company—the most critical barriers often are not outside the individual but inside.

How might McCormick have done her job with such a bias for purposeful action? We never get the sense that she really had any "personal skin" in the game—that she had taken personal responsibility for the total quality program's success. What if she had thought about, planned, implemented, and pushed the program forward with a true sense of commitment right from the start? What if, before accepting the job, she had discussed with Dermott the conditions that would allow her to make the project a success? What if, rather than filling her days with task after task, she had stopped and reflected on what she truly hoped to accomplish through the total quality project overall—and ways that she might go about doing that?

We can just imagine how different the results might have been had Laura taken this kind of purposeful action. Indeed, in our research we have seen dramatic changes occur in companies such as Lufthansa, British Petroleum, Hilti, Sony, and Oracle, whose managers show just such a bias for action—and whose organizational and leadership processes support managers' action-taking capabilities (see the appendix). Throughout this book, we will

draw on those examples to suggest how executives can help themselves and others in their organizations keep from making hasty
commitments or getting absorbed in everyday routines.

Let us begin, however, by looking at how purposeful action
works.

Action Versus Busyness: The Power of Energy and Focus

People who exhibit purposeful action possess two critical
traits: energy and focus. *Energy* implies a level of personal involvement that is more than just doing something. Rather, it is
subjectively meaningful action; it genuinely matters to the action-
taker. Energy also implies effort. The action involves a certain
amount of exertion, fueled not only by external pressures but also
by an individual's inner resources. Purposeful action, then, is self-
generated, engaged, and self-driven behavior. Laura McCormick
lacked precisely this energy in the way that she carried out her role
in the total quality project: She never really demonstrated that the
project mattered to her on a personal level. Instead, it seemed as if
she were simply going through the motions of accomplishing the
daily tasks surrounding the program.

Purposeful action is also *focused* behavior. It is conscious and
intentional, guided by a person's decision to achieve a particular
goal. It requires discipline to resist distraction, overcome problems, and persist in the face of unanticipated setbacks. In other
words, purposeful action is different from impulsive behavior; it
does not emerge from the moment but involves thought, analysis,
and planning. McCormick failed to act with this kind of focus;
she always seemed simply to react to problems rather than to act
toward clear goals.

Unfortunately, everyday managerial work is hazardous to focus,
in particular. Why? As Henry Mintzberg described so vividly in
his pioneering book *The Nature of Managerial Work*, unlike the
work of, say, a farmer or a scholar or even a software specialist,
managers typically must work on a variety of different tasks simultaneously, and they rely on help of others in the company to

get the job done—often without tangible milestones or clearly defined processes or goals. Moreover, managers face days that are rife with interruptions and unexpected demands on their time without relief—all while dealing with sometimes overwhelming time constraints.[6]

No wonder, then, that at the end of our decade-long study of executives at a dozen companies, we reached this disturbing conclusion: Despite all their activity, only a small fraction of managers actually get something done that really matters or moves their organizations forward in a meaningful way. In other words, most managers do not take purposeful action.

Four Types of Managerial Behavior

If most managers are not acting purposefully in their everyday jobs, what are they doing, and how are they carrying out their work? As we have said, purposeful management depends on energy and focus. Our research identified four kinds of managerial behavior that we plotted according to the levels of energy and focus that managers displayed.

- *The Frenzied:* Forty percent of managers are distracted by the myriad tasks that they juggle each day. They are highly energetic but very unfocused and appear to others as frenzied, desperate, and hasty.

- *The Procrastinators:* Thirty percent procrastinate on doing the work that really matters to the organization because they lack both energy and focus. They often feel insecure and fear failure.

- *The Detached:* Twenty percent of managers are disengaged or detached from their work altogether. They are focused but lack energy and often seem aloof, tense, and apathetic.

- *The Purposeful:* Only 10 percent get the job done. They are highly focused and energetic and come across as reflective and calm amid chaos.

In a moment, we will examine the characteristics of the purposeful manager, but first let us look at the type of executive that is by far the most common—and the most hazardous to themselves and the organization: the frenzied manager. These overly busy people are usually highly motivated and well intentioned. They are enthusiastic about their work, identify strongly with their jobs—and could achieve a lot if they would consciously concentrate their efforts amid the swirl of activities they juggle. The culture of speed and unreflective activity that dominates most organizations only encourages these managers' mindless busyness, inciting them to toil ceaselessly and, above all, to act without hesitation.

The costs, of course, are great for both the managers and companies. Continual, unreflective activity is costly for the individual because it is not effective and is, therefore, ultimately unsatisfying. Because these managers identify so strongly with their jobs, they tend to get frustrated or hurt more easily when confronted with setbacks, criticism, or mediocre performance. Often they have difficulties dealing with the higher effectiveness and, eventually, the greater success of their more reflective and purposeful colleagues.

Companies, too, pay the price for employing overly busy managers. Such frenzied managers—especially when under pressure or in times of crisis—are distracted managers, and they act in extremely shortsighted ways. Because they do not take time to reflect, they typically deal with immediate problems while neglecting long-term issues. They underestimate the time needed to implement a strategy, or they begin activities without analyzing the risks and long-term implications.[7] Frenzied managers demonstrate a well-intentioned but desperate need to do something—anything—making them as potentially destructive as the proverbial bull in the china shop.

Not surprisingly, many managers who are chronic procrastinators were once frenzied managers. That was the case with Laura McCormick. Before she received the total quality assignment, she was a classic frenzied manager, carrying out her daily tasks with zeal and compulsively ticking things off of her to-do lists. Her new assignment, however, pushed her into the procrastination zone. Busying herself with the daily minutiae of her job, she continually put off reflecting about what she really needed to do to make total quality a success. Lacking both focus and energy, she never really got excited about the project. It was not meaningful to her personally—which created a snowball effect in which setbacks and obstacles easily discouraged her.

Now let us look at the purposeful manager—and how that rare 10 percent gets the job done when others do not.

Willpower: The Force Behind Purposeful Action

Why are some managers highly energetic and focused, while others procrastinate, disengage, or dissipate their energy in unfocused busyness? What distinguishes managers who take purposeful action from those who do not? Most leaders would ascribe the difference to how motivated—or not—the manager feels. Laura McCormick's boss, Alan Sartora, for example, clearly thought motivation was the answer when he used flattery to encourage her to stick with the project. ("People *like* you," he told her, "and you are good.") But our research indicates that leaders need more than motivation to spur people to purposeful action.

While motivation might suffice in helping managers sustain organizational routines, managers are not generally paid just to maintain routines. Rather, their tasks are usually complex and require creativity and innovation. They often must strive for multiple and conflicting goals, many of which are long-term projects that require sustained effort. Ambitious goals, high uncertainty, extreme opposition—these circumstances underscore the limitations of motivation. Managers who make things happen under these conditions—who exhibit consistently purposeful action—rely on a different force: *the power of their will.*[8]

Willpower—the force behind energy and focus—goes a decisive step further than motivation. It enables managers to execute disciplined action, even when they are disinclined to do something, uninspired by the work, or tempted by other opportunities. An insatiable need to produce results infects willful managers.[9] They overcome barriers, deal with setbacks, and persevere to the end. With willpower, giving up is not an option; there is no way back. Willful managers resolve to achieve their intention, no matter what. Jack Welch implied this doggedness when he wrote, "I learned the most important principle of life from my mother: you just have to want it."[10]

McCormick could not harness that key force of willpower. She never demonstrated a clear moment of decision around the total quality project, she had no mental model of what she hoped to achieve, and she left herself the option to relinquish her role when the going got tough. The result? Her doubts and insecurities got the better of her, and she never really discovered what she could accomplish.

The good news is that every manager—including procrastinators like McCormick—is capable of engaging willpower. From our observations, willpower is neither limited to a certain set of personality traits, nor to a person's particular work situation. So how can managers activate and harness this powerful force in their own lives? We cannot prescribe a magic formula, but we can describe an effective process: Willpower flourishes when people develop a clear mental picture of their intention, make a conscious choice to commit to and pursue that intention, and develop strategies for protecting their intention against distractions, boredom, or frustration.

More than anyone else in the organization, top leaders must possess willpower. Without it, how can they direct or encourage others or provide meaning to their people's work? The problem is that most leaders actually end up destroying their managers' willpower by encouraging superficial acquiescence to tasks—but not real commitment to specific goals.[11]

Leaders who activate their own willpower can then engage others' willpower by doing precisely the opposite of what leaders typically do. Rather than simply motivate their people, as McCormick's boss attempted to do, leaders must create a desire for action without encouraging superficiality. Leaders must ignite people's dreams while preventing them from making hasty promises. Leaders must make commitment more difficult rather than get quick buy-ins. They must force their people to consider conflicts, doubts, anxieties, and ambivalence, and they must discuss the difficulties, costs, and privations rather than paint rosy pictures of the necessary tasks.

Is willful leadership easy or intuitive? No. But it is more effective and ultimately less risky than just motivating managers and counting on their halfhearted acceptance. Moreover, leadership that activates people's willpower involves more than simply influencing others personally. Leaders must also create an organizational context that does not suppress people's inner drive and, instead, gives it a reason to flourish—and some space in which to do so.

How to Build an Organization That Supports Purposeful Action

Leaders who seriously foster managerial willpower craft three critical conditions in their organizations: they create space for autonomous action; they build processes for providing professional, social, and emotional support; and they develop a culture that celebrates the exercise of responsible willpower. Let us briefly look at each in turn.

To exercise their willpower, managers must first have sufficient freedom to act. Developing a sense of personal ownership requires not only the space to maneuver but also an experience of that space. Clearly, Alan Sartora wished to provide that kind of freedom for Laura McCormick. Unfortunately, the processes in the organization did not truly support her taking purposeful action. In fact, most organizational processes typically foster a kind of mindless busyness.

Which brings us to the second organizational requirement: Managers need organizational processes that support unwavering action. By *support* we mean not just professional backing but also social and emotional help. Ideally, managers will have supervisors who inspire and encourage them, as well as informal relationships with peers and mentors who provide professional support—the information and resources that managers need to accomplish their work. They also need emotional support—a context in which people in the organization help each other cope with stress and leverage powerful emotions.[12]

Organizational structures and management processes by themselves, however, cannot create and sustain willful action over long periods. In most companies, the rhetoric of leaders emphasizes empowerment and celebrates autonomous action of managers, but the reality is often exactly the opposite. Companies like those need to build supportive cultures—the final principle for designing an organization that facilitates willful action. Again, this is what McCormick lacked at IBG—where instead of feeling supported she felt like a victim of internal power struggles and political agendas. To unleash the willpower of their managers, leaders absolutely must embed purposeful behavior as a central element of the company's core values and shared understanding of how it does business. Ultimately, that kind of organizational culture stimulates and sustains managers' courage to exercise choice and their ability to enjoy freedom.

While the requirements of autonomy, support, and a culture that encourages willpower are straightforward, effectively developing those qualities is less intuitive. Personal freedom and shared support are difficult to combine. Highly autonomous managers focus only on their own tasks and tend not to share knowledge with others, or to invest their own energy into helping others succeed. No quick fixes, then, can create a culture of sustainable willful action in an organization; it results from a long journey of continuously demanding the values of purposeful action and personal responsibility. Yet, leadership that is courageous, persistent, and patient can reconcile these tensions. As we will illustrate in part II of this book, leaders have several strategies to move both individual managers and their organizations as a whole toward a bias for action.

But first, by learning to identify and understand the traps of nonaction, individual managers themselves can harness their willpower to become more purposeful. Let us now continue part I with this examination of managerial behavior by taking a closer look at two central drivers of purposeful action—energy and focus—and how they relate to our four types of managers.

Distinguishing Purposeful Action from Active Nonaction

E XECUTIVES OFTEN SAY that their most crucial job is to see the big picture—to grapple with strategic issues, to reduce costs, to surmount new markets, to beat new competitors. So why do these same executives rush from meeting to meeting, check e-mail constantly, return phone call after phone call in an astonishing flurry of nonstop activity?

No doubt, executives are under incredible pressure to perform, and they have far too much to do. But the fact is, very few managers use their time as effectively as they could. While some think that they are attending to pressing matters—but are really just stamping out fires—most managers are in fact aware of their unproductive busyness and bemoan the problem.

What is the difference between being active and taking purposeful action? Managers who take effective action—those who make the seemingly impossible happen—rely on a combination of two critical aspects of executive work: energy and focus. We think of energy as exertion or vigor deriving from intense personal involvement, and focus as concentrated attention. By plotting the two dimensions of energy and focus against each other, we discovered a powerful framework for understanding the causes of active nonaction and the sources of purposeful action that correspond with the four types of managerial behavior: the procrastinators, the detached, the frenzied, and the purposeful (see figure 2-1).

While we all want to see organizations full of purposeful action-takers, most managerial behavior falls into one of the three other quadrants. By understanding behavior in this context, managers can identify the common dynamics underlying their own active nonaction, recognize such behavior when they see or do it, and pinpoint the causes.

Before we explore each type of behavior individually, let us look at how energy and focus combine into purposeful action—the most powerful form of managerial behavior.

FIGURE 2-1

Focus, Energy, and the Four Managerial Behaviors

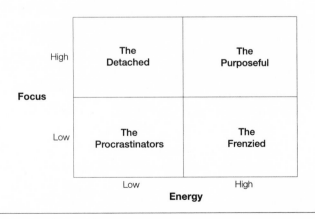

Energy and Focus

Energy is vigor fueled by intense personal commitment and involvement. Energy gets things going. As anyone who has participated in competitive sports knows, energy is the emotional tenacity that can release immense inner resources when the stakes are high.[1] In business, energy allows quick and effective action in high-pressure situations.

The team that created the Sony VAIO computer displayed just such energy when it crafted the first PC to let users combine other Sony products and services, such as digital cameras, camcorders, and portable music systems.[2] Responding to CEO Nobuyuki Idei's challenge to create an integrated technological platform to provide home entertainment to the burgeoning generation of kids with digital dreams, Hiroshi Nakagawa and his team put in 100-hour weeks to create the kind of breakthrough product that Idei had hoped for. One manager, Kazumasa Sato, was so committed to the project that he spent every weekend for three years observing customers in the electronics shops of Tokyo's Akihabara neighborhood. The insights he developed into consumer buying patterns helped Sony create a shop layout that enhanced traffic flows and, ultimately, sales of the PC. In the end, VAIO captured a significant share in Japan's highly competitive PC market.

The Sony team illustrates three critical elements of energetic behavior. First, energy requires that the action be subjectively meaningful.[3] Managers do many things, but they put energy only into those projects that mean something to them personally—as the VAIO project clearly did for the team at Sony.

Second, energy implies that managers take proactive action and initiative. Their need to act comes from within—as it did for Kazumasa Sato during all of those weekends he spent in electronics shops.[4] Energy leads managers to develop goals and initiate actions, rather than to be constrained by situational requirements. With energy, managers shape their environment and create the context they need to reach their objectives.

Finally, energy is what pushes managers to make exceptional efforts when tackling heavy workloads or responding to tight deadlines. That kind of energy drove the VAIO team members to work 100-hour weeks until they achieved their objective. Energy is the source of managers' stamina for pursuing ambitious goals, and it implies an accelerated speed and heightened intensity of work. Energetic managers are more present—their increased attention levels activate more of their inner physical, intellectual, and emotional resources, which, in turn, help them achieve extraordinary things. Energy is the source of persistence that allows managers to achieve long-term goals.

The other critical element of purposeful action—*focus*—is essentially energy channeled toward a specific outcome. Focused managers can concentrate even amid the many distractions that flare up every day.

Take, for example, the steely discipline and dedicated focus of Thomas Sattelberger. Now an executive board member at Continental AG, Sattelberger realized his dream of creating Germany's first corporate university, the Lufthansa School of Business, in the 1990s when he was a senior human resource manager at Lufthansa. His case illustrates three conditions that managers must fulfill to develop focused behavior.

First, rather than merely reacting to developments as they arise, or meeting routine requirements, focused managers are goal oriented. They have clear ideas about what they are striving for.[5] Back in the late 1980s, Sattelberger first conceived of the corporate university as a place where managers could challenge the status quo and learn techniques to shake up the organization's operational practices. When unbridgeable gaps between the strategic orientation of the CEO at his former employer—one of the country's largest industrial groups—and his vision became obvious, Sattelberger joined Lufthansa. There, despite the high demands of a senior HR role, he mustered the time and effort to pitch his project to top management. That is the goal-orientation requirement of focus: Activities are directed toward a clear purpose.

Second, focus requires that a manager is intentional, channeling all activities toward achieving the desired goal.[6] That means taking the time to reflect regularly on your own behavior, and being willing and able to choose what you do and do not do each day. Focused behavior does not emerge by chance, nor from the moment.[7] It requires planning and strategic foresight to ensure intentionality. Sattelberger did not merely dream of the Lufthansa School of Business. He prepared a detailed business case that linked the project with Lufthansa's larger transformational agenda, and he systematically acted in pursuit of his goal.

Third, focus requires personal discipline. That means protecting yourself against the usual noise of everyday demands—or exciting opportunities—that will inevitably tug at your attention and emotions. It also means not allowing resistance to keep you from pursuing your goal. Sattelberger faced much resistance indeed when he first joined Lufthansa. For one thing, the company was in the midst of a cost-cutting program; a long-term investment to build a corporate university was simply not a priority for top management. Moreover, the airline's human resource processes and structures were in sad shape. Sattelberger knew that to realize his dream, he would first have to get the right systems in place. For two years, then, he worked to clean up HR, all the while keeping sight of his goal to create a university. Steadily, he chipped away at management's reservations—and his focus paid off: In 1998, four years after Sattelberger joined the airline, the Lufthansa School of Business opened its doors as Germany's first corporate university.

Clearly, a high level of focus also has its drawbacks. Determination can degenerate into stubbornness. Focused managers can become blind to the consequences of their own actions—and insensitive to others' goals. Too much focus—without a high level of energy to balance it—can lead to inflexibility, narrow-mindedness, or mental inertia. It can also harm people: Managers really focused on particular goals but lacking the energy to pursue them are candidates for burnout.[8] At the same time, high energy without focus is likely to dissipate in purposeless busyness. Worse still, energetic managers lacking focus can seriously harm the organization through their highly vigorous—but poorly considered—activities.[9]

In our study of a wide variety of companies, we encountered managers with diverse combinations of both dimensions: those with low levels of both energy and focus—the procrastinators; those high on one dimension and low on the other—the detached and the frenzied; and those with high levels of both energy and focus—the purposeful.

Fortunately, our observations suggest that certain behavior modifications can move all types of managers toward the kind of bias for action that helps organizations thrive. But first, let us take a closer look at each managerial behavior.

The Procrastinators: Low Energy, Low Focus

Beth Brown, a young lawyer at a large U.S.-based oil corporation, had just landed a key role in an innovative merger project that the company had entered. The stakes were high, and all eyes would witness her first presentation to the executive board. But rather than working on her presentation, Brown kept finding ways to displace her energy into mundane tasks. It was not that she was uninspired; in fact, she was excited about the project and felt challenged by her new role. But whenever she set aside time to work on it, she was overcome with negative feelings, worrying that her ideas would fall flat and the presentation would flop. Finally, the night before the presentation, when she could no longer put it off, Brown managed to throw something together—and though it was not the disaster she had imagined, it was certainly less polished than it might have been had she gotten started earlier.

About 30 percent of the managers we studied failed to take purposeful action simply because, like Brown, they hesitated— lacking both the energy and focus necessary to drive change. These procrastinators continued to perform routine tasks—attending meetings, writing memos, making phone calls, and so on. But all the while they failed to take initiative when it came to starting new projects, raising performance levels, or engaging in strategic change and chose instead to continue their busywork.

Procrastination comes in several varieties, we found.[10] Beth Brown's is a classic case of an executive who, despite her personal excitement about the project, displaced both her energy and focus because she was unclear even how to begin. She also feared that once she did begin, she would never live up to her own perfectionist standards. So, she simply avoided preparing her presentation until she could no longer put off it.[11] Another group of managers postponed projects for the exact opposite reason: Their work was not exciting or challenging enough. They would typically hesitate, Hamlet-like, until the opportunity to seize the moment no longer existed.

A third group of managers procrastinated because they simply coasted along in a state of what psychologist Martin Seligman called "learned helplessness"—a persistent feeling that any effort is hopeless because it will eventually hit a wall.[12] This form of hesitation, based on a deeply internalized perception of lack of control (often the result of repeated negative experiences with taking action), is one of the most harmful, debilitating types of active nonaction in companies. Believing that nothing they do will effect change, managers become frustrated and gradually withdraw their energy and focus—eventually saying to themselves, "Why bother?" The result is a cadre of employees who simply go through the motions of work—but never try to make anything happen.

The Detached: Low Energy, High Focus

Charles Wagner, the manager of quality control at a major manufacturer where he had worked for a decade, knew that his company was in serious financial trouble. If it were to survive, it needed to enact radical change across the organization—including staff cuts in Wagner's own department. But while he participated in the meetings about change management and contributed ideas that would improve the company's productivity, Wagner never really allowed the discussions to really reach him; he did not internalize the implications of the concepts and ideas. He simply did not make the emotional link between the general needed change and what it meant for his own department. In fact, deep in his heart Wagner believed that his job was to protect his people. Although he intellectually agreed on the need for change, he could not stand behind it emotionally. When eventually it became clear that across-the-board layoffs were unavoidable, Wagner agreed to make the cuts. He carried out every change activity responsibly and in a focused way. His personal discomfort was apparent to everyone, however; his day-to-day demeanor seemed almost listless, devoid of all energy.

About 20 percent of managers we studied exhibited, as Wagner did, low levels of energy accompanied by high levels of focus in their jobs. Some of them were simply exhausted and lacked the inner resources to reenergize themselves. For others, their low energy related to specific projects that somehow were not meaningful to them. Because this group of managers had reservations about what they were being asked to do, they performed their tasks halfheartedly.

One manifestation of this state of mind is defensive avoidance, which allows managers to perpetuate patterns of behavior that they have refined over long periods of time.[13] Instead of acknowledging a problem and taking steps to correct it, they convince themselves that the problem does not exist. They focus exclusively on legitimizing their position and spend all their resources finding justifications for denying reality. But the high-focus, low-energy combination also expresses itself in the form of disengaged doing—the urge to distance oneself personally from the action—that we saw when Charles Wagner could no longer avoid cutting his staff.

Detached managers often further deplete their own energy by trying to maintain the status quo—which can actually be very stressful, for two reasons. First, disengaged behavior is driven by the inability to cope with strong emotions—anxiety, uncertainty, anger, frustration, and alienation—coupled with an inner withdrawal from productive action opportunities. Detached managers live in a defensive state, aligned with neither their job requirements nor with the tasks necessary for carrying those requirements out. Most of their energy goes into acknowledging their own powerful emotions and legitimizing their nonaction to themselves and others, creating a lot of tension indeed. Second, detached managers create stress because they usually react rather than act. Unlike purposeful managers who engage their energy to be proactive self-starters, as reactors, detached managers cannot plan and implement their activities independently. They tend to do only what others demand; the unexpected easily overwhelms them. Despite their low energy, then, detached managers suffer far more from burnout than their energetic colleagues do.

The Frenzied: High Energy, Low Focus

When senior management at a global high-tech firm decided that the company had to reduce costs, some managers became frenetic doers. Janet Hill, an IT manager who had been with the company eight years, found herself single-mindedly pursuing the goal to create savings but—as she admitted herself—"not always using [her] brain." After immediately cutting people who were nice to have but not crucial, she did not stop there. She kept issuing pink slips, letting people go who were actually vital to the firm's future, experts who knew how to craft solutions when they were needed or to make critical purchasing decisions. "We later had to hire back some of these people," Hill told us, "and at higher salaries. I was dominated by the feeling that something had to happen quickly, so I saw only one objective—not the whole picture."

By far the largest group of managers we studied—more than 40 percent—were busy managers like Janet Hill who confuse frenetic energy with constructive action. Especially when under pressure or during a crisis, their actions frequently produce inefficient, misdirected, even damaging results.

One manifestation of busyness is a habitual, frenetic shortsightedness.[14] Managers with such shortsightedness develop new behavioral strategies, but without proper reflection and internalization, they can make costly mistakes. While managers are more likely to fall victim to this kind of thoughtless activism in a crisis, the behavior is by no means limited to such situations.[15] Even when the organization is relatively stable, some managers create their own crisis, drive themselves and others into a state of frenzy, and experience enormous pressure for no good reason. These kinds of managers perceive that they are under constant time constraints. Feeling that everything is urgent, they do not prioritize. The result? Shortsighted strategies and impulsive activity that solve immediate problems while neglecting long-term issues.

Frenzied managers also tend to engage in habitual, and sometimes ineffective, patterns of behavior.[16] Especially in times of crisis, these managers intuitively use ingrained ways of doing things—such as carrying out processes that no longer reflect the company's new needs—when instead they should take time to reflect on how they might do things differently. And even when they do reflect and devise a new strategy, they often forget their plan when the next crisis flares up.

Finally, one particularly seductive kind of busyness is thematic straying, or grasshopping.[17] In the excitement of the moment, some managers get involved in several different projects, with no clear sense of priority. This particular phenomenon often emerges when, without taking time to reflect, the manager focuses exclusively on the benefits of a particular outcome—while forgetting to take the costs into consideration. Other managers fall into this grasshopping behavior simply because they have trouble saying no. Inevitably, thematic strayers eventually lose focus or interest and end up either constantly fighting fires or abandoning the projects they adopted in their original euphoria.

The Purposeful: High Energy, High Focus

Back in the early 1990s, when Lufthansa airlines was on the brink of bankruptcy, one middle manager we interviewed in human resources, whom we will call Gerhard Schneider, was offered the unpleasant but crucial job of joining a change task force that would coordinate and monitor 132 operations projects designed to turn the company around.[18] A fifteen-year veteran of the company, Schneider was known as a gifted communicator who was very creative and often worked overtime to complete his assignments. But participating in the task force and monitoring the change projects could spawn some serious power struggles with the people who were responsible for implementing those projects. Schneider's job would involve pressuring line managers to complete their work on time and pointing out problems that arose. As the board member who offered him the position made clear: "Doing this job successfully might mean that you have made so many people unhappy that you will have to leave the company." Did he still want the job? For a few days, Schneider struggled with the decision. "But then, it became clear," he told us. "I had to join the task force. The company had to be saved, and I had no choice but to succeed." The airline's successful turnaround two years later was a testament to his conviction.

Making such deliberate choices can often be a difficult, even painful process, but purposeful managers—about 10 percent of those we studied—often do so as a matter of course. Unlike those who hesitate, avoid, or overreact, we found that purposeful managers embody a special combination of the two dimensions of focus and energy. Not only does their energy level exceed that of most people, they are also extremely focused on achieving their goals. Moreover, like Gerhard Schneider, these people tend to exhibit a strong sense of personal significance, an ability to thrive in chaos, and an ability to step back and reflect.

While others had difficulties in articulating the goals of their actions, purposeful managers whom we interviewed at Lufthansa attached high significance to their individual work, even when their goals were not strictly defined. They were convinced that they were needed and were contributing to something big and meaningful. They felt a sense of personal responsibility for the company's fate, and that feeling anchored the purposefulness of their actions. Indeed, these managers referred to their contribution to Lufthansa's turnaround in the stark vocabulary of life and death: They were "fighting for survival," "staunching the loss of blood," or providing "first aid" to the corporate body.

Purposeful managers also appear more self-aware than most people. Their clarity about their intentions, combined with discipline, helps them make careful, high-quality decisions about where and how they spend their time. They pick their goals—and their battles—with far more deliberation than other managers we studied. Moreover, purposeful executives do not shrink from challenges or hide behind make-work; rather, they eagerly assume responsibility. To the managers whom we observed, undefined demands and big questions provided a welcome opportunity to take initiative, to innovate, and to push their projects quickly forward.[19] One Lufthansa executive responsible for reducing travel agencies' commissions told us, "I developed the philosophy, 'When nobody is responsible, I am responsible. I can own the issue and do what I think is necessary.' I acted accordingly—unless and until [CEO] Jürgen Weber pulled me back."

The Lufthansa case might imply that purposeful managers respond well only when facing a crisis, or even that crisis is what creates purposeful action. On the contrary, we found that many of these managers did not throttle down once the turbulence of the airline's turnaround had eased. One person, for example, played a key role in managing Programm 15, a strategic cost-saving plan launched in 1996, soon after the press reported the turnaround's success. Following his conviction that, to sustain success, the company must continue cost saving, he led this initially unpopular project to reduce the cost of seats per kilometer from 17.7 pfennig

(10.3 cents) in 1996 to 15 pfennig (8.7 cents) in 2001—resulting in an overall cost reduction of 20 percent.

Why do some managers succeed in taking purposeful action while others do not? In part, the answer lies in personal dispositions. Some people just have more energy than others; some lack focus while others tend to be more disciplined by nature.[20] But this is only part of the story. Everyone is capable of enhancing his or her action-taking ability. In the next chapter, we will meet people who deliberately reshaped their personal behavior by reenergizing themselves or renewing focus in their work.

Marshaling Energy and Developing Focus

K nowing a purposeful manager when you see one is much easier than transforming yourself into a purposeful manager,
especially when you have somehow devolved into a frenzied doer
or a chronic procrastinator—or have become detached from your
job altogether.

How can managers harness the necessary energy and focus to
succeed and, equally important, to engage fully in their work? By
developing a potent combination of strategies that includes defining their goal and mastering techniques for overcoming negativity
(for energy), and then learning ways to visualize that goal (for
focus). In this chapter, we identify specific ways to move toward
purposeful action-taking and meet two real managers who did
just that.

Let us begin with the first key task of energizing yourself and
your work.

Marshaling Energy: Defining Your Challenge and Overcoming Negativity

What does a manager need to build and sustain energy for purposeful action-taking? In our study, executives who regained their personal energy did so through two important processes: finding a clear, ambitious goal that they felt confident about achieving and then actively managing their emotions relating to the tasks needed to achieve that goal.[1] That emotion management includes both deliberately stopping counterproductive behaviors and consciously regaining positive task-related behaviors.[2]

Finding Your Goal

Goals have an enormously energizing effect on people, particularly when they are clear and well defined, and when they are ambitious enough to be challenging yet not so unrealistic that they're paralyzing.[3] Clear, challenging goals offer people a sense of meaning and direction, and they help sustain people through the effort needed for achieving them.

You cannot simply have a goal, however; you must also personally believe that you can achieve it. This belief is not about having the necessary skills and competencies: Many competent people fail to develop energy and take purposeful action. It means having the confidence that you can cope with the particular challenges and demands associated with the goal, and that you can meet your own and others' expectations for the project. This confidence can come from many different sources.[4] It might result from a training program in which you learn strategies for seeing the big picture. It can come from researching your fields of interest and gathering data to make thoughtful, informed choices. Most often, such a subjective belief in your own ability to accomplish a task comes from a role model, or past experiments and experiences that helped you develop clarity about your strengths and weaknesses.

When defining a worthwhile goal, then, try using the following guidelines:

- *Choose a goal that is well defined and concrete.* You will need to have an exact understanding of what components the goal entails, as well as the hurdles you will need to leap in order to reach it.
- *Choose a goal with which you can personally identify.* You must believe that pursuing it is worthwhile, given your own values, and you must believe in its overall merit for the organization.
- *Set a goal that feels personally challenging.* You should feel stretched by it, but not so overwhelmed that you cannot take the first step to reach it. Your goal must feel achievable, or else you will soon abandon it.

Defining your goal, however, is only one requirement for energizing your work. The second component is equally important: identifying and overcoming any negative reactions to strong emotions, and then developing positive responses that support your intentions and goals.

Clearing Negativity and Leveraging Strong Emotions

Detached managers, in particular, often suffer from overwhelming thoughts and feelings. Since they tend to simply suppress those feelings—literally swallow them—rather than deal with them, these managers often appear continually anxious and stressed, or even burned out or paralyzed. Having no outlet for that tension—no tools for expressing, understanding, and managing it—their repression saps their energy for doing any real constructive work. Both detached and procrastinating managers often have an associated but distinct problem: They are driven by negative reactions to their feelings and lack the positive emotional fuel needed for energetic action. Rather than actively managing their emotions, they become victims of their emotions. The result? What begins as fear and anger soon becomes frustration and resignation. Somewhere along the line, these people cease to feel truly connected to their work and instead begin simply going through the motions.

Again, training programs can often provide just the tonic for injecting enthusiasm into bored, disenfranchised executives. But whether through a formal program or one that you create yourself, you must learn ways to manage negative responses to your emotions and the stress that such negativity breeds.

When Lufthansa underwent its transformation in the early 1990s—as well as between 2001 and 2003 when the airline dealt with the crises following 9-11, the SARS virus, and the Iraq war—every manager confronted painful tasks under difficult circumstances.[5] Most of them experienced a substantially increased workload and long-term strain as well as a very high level of emotional tension and pressure. Some of these managers fell victim to a gradual but inevitable erosion of their emotional energy. Others, however, found ways to reenergize themselves and thus continue to pursue their projects.

How could these managers sustain their emotional force? They relied on two simple but effective mechanisms.[6] First, they appeared to have a valve for regulating the flow of their emotions. They knew exactly how to process their painful emotions and inner tensions. For some it was an intensive sport that helped them let off emotional steam. Others relied on the help of a personal "crying wall"—their partner, a good friend, or a colleague with whom they could share their fears, frustrations, and inner burdens. Most of them could name certain locations or activities that helped them cope with their strong emotions. One manager told us about his garden, which had a strong stabilizing effect on him. During difficult periods he spent long hours there, often talking to himself about what bothered him. He knew that gardening would restore his inner balance so that he could plan his next steps.

Second, most of these Lufthansa managers had a "personal well"—a distinct source of positive energy—from which they could draw for regular replenishment. Personal wells could be anything from a hobby to a special place that had a reenergizing effect, but they all shared certain characteristics: They were associated with positive experiences as well as with a comprehensive—physical, emotional, and mental—sense of well-being. For some, drawing from their well was part of their mental and emotional preparation for difficult tasks. Others went to their well to energize themselves for certain ambitious milestones or to get through a difficult phase of a project. Overall, the well served two purposes: It was a reliable source of positive energy, and it was a source of emotional strength, a place to refuel.

If you find yourself suffering from low energy, try refueling through regular sports or hobbies. Or build a nurturing network of friends and supporters with whom you can process some of your workplace anxiety. By deliberately engaging in activities that create positive reactions to emotions at work, you will gradually overcome thoughts and behaviors that once fueled your negativity. You will create a personal well from which you can draw energy. Purposeful action-takers know exactly what their source of positive energy is. The very knowledge that such a well exists serves as a source of comfort and stability. They also have a repertoire of specific positive ways to deal with painful or uncomfortable emotions.

Of course, just because you have made changes in how you approach your emotions does not mean that your work environment will magically change as well. Your job may continue to be just as chaotic and unstructured as ever. But by replacing negative responses with positive ones, you will find a new source of energy in yourself: a product of the coming together of a specific, meaningful, and ambitious goal; a renewed confidence in your ability to achieve the goal; and mastery of caring, constructive ways of experiencing difficult emotions. Those are the requirements for developing and protecting the energy essential for purposeful action-taking on the job.

But how does all of this work in practice? Let us look at what happened to Klaus Karl, a manager on the brink of quitting his job, when he reenergized himself with a clear and ambitious goal—and learned to manage his emotions.

From Detached to Purposeful: Klaus Karl's Story

In 1995 Klaus Karl, a young software engineer in the relational-database section of the middleware division at Siemens Nixdorf Informationssysteme (SNI), had reached the end of his rope.[7] His company verged on collapse, facing cumulative five-year losses of 2.1 billion deutsche marks (about $1.3 billion U.S.) and a progressive erosion of the market. Karl's relational-database business was losing so much money that rumors spread about outsourcing it to the main supplier. Internally, the vastly different corporate cultures of two merger partners (Nixdorf computers and the computer division of Siemens) had created a politically vicious, unstable environment—a perfect breeding ground for procrastination and detachment.

Exhausted by the political battles and the apparent hopelessness of the company's financial situation, Karl grew apathetic. He had long before stopped feeling challenged by his work. Now, with the turbulent new business environment, he could not define a concrete goal to pursue. Although he kept hoping that his superiors would provide him with such a goal—and challenging tasks to go with it—instead he got continual uncertainty: His job—and his bosses—changed three times in nine months. "What I saw in the first phase of the merger was a cloud of dust," he said. "It was complete chaos. I had no idea of my goals or priorities. I was completely lost. What I was expecting was more structure, more stability, but instead what I experienced was more uncertainty, more flux."

Karl knew that he needed to take an active stand in managing his job, but he became reactive, stressed, and overwhelmed by the ceaseless stream of new information and job requirements. Without trusted relationships either with his colleagues or superiors, how could he hope to see the big picture of his career? Feeling paralyzed about what to do next, Karl felt his only option was to leave the company. So when he received a good offer from Sybase, a software manufacturer, he felt he could not refuse.

Then something happened that changed everything. With his departure date less than a month away, Klaus Karl attended a meeting organized by SNI's newly hired CEO, Gerhard Schulmeyer. In that meeting, Schulmeyer sounded a call for action. He reminded them of the company's European roots, saying that it was destined to be a far better technology partner to companies on the Continent than any U.S. competitor could possibly be. Dubbing the company "the IT partner for change," Schulmeyer announced that he would give its technology-savvy young people a chance to take part in corporate strategic planning. Their challenge? To help top management rethink SNI's approach to the market, to technology, and to change. Karl's name was on the list of star employees chosen to join the new team.

For the first time in years, Karl felt truly challenged, shaken from his apathy by Schulmeyer's speech. "I faced a real dilemma," said Karl. "I had an excellent offer, with higher pay and great prospects. My boss [at SNI] told me that the change effort would most likely fail and that I might find myself looking for a job." But Schulmeyer also offered an exciting proposition: If Karl accepted a role in the change agent project, he would join Schulmeyer and other top managers at a three-month management training program at MIT in the United States—after which Karl could define his own change initiative. When Karl weighed his options, the chance to make a difference proved too alluring to pass up. He committed to SNI.

During the training program in the United States, Karl acquired a repertoire of strategy and change management tools. He made friends in the program and began to forge close bonds with them. By the time the program ended, Karl and his fellow trainees —as well as Schulmeyer—were committed to transforming the company. Karl also acquired a durable confidence. Before the course, he was focused on his area of responsibility and was often surprised by broader company developments. That made him insecure about his ability to take initiative and to shape and manage change.[8] He could not trust his own judgments, and that insecurity exhausted him. After the course, Karl told us, "[I had] a very complete overview of all the aspects of the business. I felt I could understand the business and knew why certain things went as they did . . . and I [could] develop an agenda for myself."

Karl also developed a new style of working during the program. He learned how to take his mind off work, reenergize himself, and return to the job fully refreshed—a new skill for someone who had always driven himself relentlessly, with few outlets for the accumulated stress and tension. Before, anxiety had often dominated his work, and worries drained his energy.[9] Moreover, he had not forged any stable personal bonds with superiors or colleagues who could have helped him cope with stress and anxiety. Because these intense emotions affected his life outside work as well, his home life did not provide opportunities for him to regenerate either. Besides being permanently tense, Klaus Karl lacked a source of positive excitement, a personal goal to which he was emotionally committed. His work never felt "fun."

The MIT program helped Karl discover how enjoyable intense work could be. He saw what he could do and how much he could achieve when he made a real effort. He also learned how to combine intensive work with relaxation—indeed, he discovered that instead of being at odds, the two could actually reinforce each other. Whereas in the past he might have ended each day by holing up in his room with the next day's readings, he learned to first take some time off to relax after a full day of classes. "I would join my classmates in the bar—or perhaps go out in the bitter cold of Boston and have a snowball fight," he told us. "Then I would eat and sleep, get up very early in the morning, and read. I realized that I really liked that combination. It recharges my battery. I sleep better. I work better the next day. Now it has become a part of how I live my life."

Through the MIT program Karl built a new network of relationships that later helped him cope with negative experiences at work. Where he once had tried to solve his problems alone, he now had a trusted group of cohorts with whom he could talk through his worries, share his anxieties, and develop strategies to deal with uncertainty.[10] Open conversations, jokes, and joint experiences with these trusted colleagues helped him to regain energy and to distance himself from energy-draining incidents and paralyzing depression.[11]

By learning to deal with stress and diffuse tension—and responding positively to all his emotions—Karl had already met one main requirement for reenergizing himself. Finding a goal that truly challenged his new skills as a change agent also helped.

Hans-Peter Eitel, the strategic planning manager of the middle-ware division, identified Karl as someone who could help him implement a key new strategic planning process. Together with a third team member, their work would comprise two parts: first, implementing the process and, second, providing the strategic planning support function for the middleware unit on a regular year-round basis. "Hans-Peter made a quick impression on me," said Karl. "After only a few minutes, I knew that he would be a great colleague. The job that he offered, the implementation of the strategic planning process, challenged me and seemed like a real change agent assignment."

At last, Karl had found a worthwhile goal—one that had the three characteristics that would help him transform from a passive and detached manager into one with a bias for action.[12] First, the goal was well defined and concrete. Karl had *an exact understanding of the tasks* and the contribution he would make to the change process. He knew that he had three months to obtain a clear decision on what products the company needed to drop. He was no longer merely meeting the expectations of others; rather, he was engaged in achieving a set of specific results.

Second, Karl had *a goal with which he could identify.* His efforts were subjectively meaningful because he was convinced of the necessity to transform SNI's bureaucratic structure and product-focused management. He believed that unless the product portfolio was drastically pruned, and the company's resources and priorities were refocused, the business would collapse, and that conviction enabled him to maintain his commitment throughout the implementation process. Finally, Karl found his goal *personally challenging.* It was ambitious but one that he now believed he could achieve. The knowledge he had acquired at MIT (along with his positive experience of meeting the challenges of the program) and the feedback he received from valued role models such as Eitel enhanced that confidence.

This stretching, meaningful, and concrete goal—together with Karl's renewed confidence in his ability to achieve it—created the commitment and mental strength that were key to his personal revitalization. He had regained his energy and enthusiasm for his job. He felt proud of being responsible for such an important part of the change process, and he enjoyed the time pressure and the risks. Before he often felt exhausted by the end of the day; now he enjoyed hard work and long hours. He felt strong enough to deal with setbacks and obstacles. And rather than suppressing emotions, he had developed mechanisms to cope actively with his worries, frustrations, and anxieties. Klaus Karl had effectively transformed himself from a reactive, disengaged manager to a proactive person with clear goals and the confidence and emotional strength to pursue them.

BOX 3-1

To Jump-Start Your Energy . . .

Define your goal.
   Ask yourself:

- Do I need a mentor who helps me see the big picture? Can I attend some seminars to learn such strategies? Or, do I need more information? Can I do any research to gather the data I will need to make a thoughtful, informed choice about my goals and objectives?

- Is my goal well defined and concrete? Do I understand the components my goal entails, as well as the potential obstacles to achieving it?

- Can I personally identify with my goal? Is it a worthwhile pursuit, given my own values and those of my organization?

- Does my goal feel personally challenging? Is it achievable? Will it stretch me while not overwhelming me?

Strengthen your confidence in your ability to achieve your goals.
   Ask yourself:

- What experiences with achieving comparable goals or mastering similar challenges have I made? Can I do it again?

Note that this radical transformation did not come from a change of job or work environment.[13] His job was just as chaotic and unstructured as ever. He experienced many setbacks and strong opposition, and he did not always have an immediate superior who supported or inspired him. Karl's new energy came entirely from within himself.

Over the next two years, Karl proceeded to completely shake up middleware. "We had to focus on a smaller portfolio of projects, so as to allocate our resources better," he says. "Initially, we tried to

---

- What role model do I know who helps me understand what it actually takes to achieve my goal?

- Who can give me feedback and help me evaluate whether I have the capacities to achieve my goal? What abilities do I have, and what do I have to learn to become sure that I will succeed?

- Can I experiment and rehearse certain critical tasks while pursuing my goals?

Overcome negativity, and develop positive thoughts and feelings.
Ask yourself:

- What emotions do I harbor, and what triggers them? Should I change my tasks or goals so that my work is less stressful? Do I have regular healthy outlets—hobbies, a network of friends—for these feelings?

- What about my work creates enthusiasm, fun, and excitement in me? What do I love doing? How can I consistently leverage emotions positively at work? What kind of activities do I enjoy? Whom do I like working with? Apart from my work, what is my personal well from which I can regularly draw for balance or strength?

---

persuade people to use a new set of analytical tools. They would laugh at us. Some walked away from the meetings. Many senior people even refused to attend." But Karl stuck to his guns and continued his campaign of persuasion. "Gradually, people began to listen. They began to alter their ways of thinking about projects."

As a result, a new product-portfolio analysis system was completed in a mere three months. And, thanks to the renewed energy of Karl and his fellow change agents, within three years SNI launched a variety of new projects that boosted the bottom line by 400 million deutsche marks ($240 million U.S.).

Klaus Karl's was a story of losing and then regaining energy. He already possessed the other crucial ingredient for purposeful management—focus. He only needed energy to redirect his management style toward a true bias for action.

But what of frenzied managers whose dearth of focus makes them appear constantly distracted, always doing things but never really getting anything done? Or procrastinators who are both unfocused and lacking in energy, not acting in a purposeful way because they fear failing? Let us look now at what becoming a more focused manager requires and then examine one unfocused executive who committed herself to a new direction at her company.

Focus: The Ability to Visualize and the Courage to Commit

If you saw yourself in our descriptions of the frenzied manager or the procrastinator, then you probably lack a sense of personal focus on your work. Maybe you perform your daily routine satisfactorily—answering e-mails, attending meetings, and so on—but when starting new projects or engaging in a critical strategic change, you feel overwhelmed. So you dither and dawdle, setting yourself up to fail by scrambling at the last minute. Or maybe you have no trouble getting started, but when you hit the first rock in your path, you give up. Or perhaps you have so much to do that you literally have no time to think. All day you put out fires, continually deferring real, constructive steps toward an important organizational objective. Clearly, such unfocused wheel spinning is not only bad for business; it is toxic for you. Who wants to toil away at a job that lacks a worthy purpose or deeper meaning?

Fortunately, we have watched many managers gain traction and begin making real progress in their work. How did they do it? First, they created a vivid mental picture of what they wanted to achieve, and, second, they staked their jobs on a personal commitment to that vision.

Visualizing the Intention

Focus begins when you simplify your goal or intention into a vivid mental picture. Say, for example, you hope to help your company roll out a particular new product. What might that product look like? In what kinds of stores or through what kinds of Internet venues would it sell? Can you picture the kind of customer who would typically use the product? The point is that you must visualize what you want to accomplish.

This picture, more than anything else, will allow you to sustain purposefulness, intentionality, and discipline through the action-taking phase. The clearer and more vivid your picture, the stronger your passion and personal attachment to the goal. Vivid pictures are especially important for staying committed to long-term objectives.[14] If you hit a roadblock or begin to doubt yourself, then the mental image of your goal can help sustain you.

You also need a concrete mental model of ways to enact that intention.[15] If you have trouble getting started on new projects, such a mental model might help, preparing you to exploit opportunities as they arise to inch you toward your goal. So, if your goal is to roll out a new product, then you should not only imagine what the product and its customers look like, but also see yourself performing a set of five actions, for example, to bring that product to market. That way, you can jump when the right opportunity presents itself. A model of specific actions also prepares you mentally and emotionally to overcome the inevitable speed bumps. Experienced top athletes use this strategy, maximizing their focus before a competition by imagining the potential obstacles—and picturing how they will overcome those obstacles.[16] Focused managers do the same. They visualize potential problems and incorporate those problems into their mental model for implementing their intention. Ideally, you would also define exactly when or under what conditions you would begin working toward your intention. For example, you might decide to present your new product idea just after the company announces its new growth strategy.

Crafting a vivid mental image and a model for action, however, will not alone maintain the steely focus needed for purposeful action-taking. You must also develop the courage to commit to your intention.

Making a Personal Commitment

Ultimately, managers who want to cultivate a bias for action must take full responsibility for their intentions or goals. That means recognizing that you—and not some amorphous collective "management"—determine the final outcome. Without this kind of personal commitment, you will easily go astray or else blame others for setbacks.

You can make such a commitment only when your intellectual assessment of your job aligns with your own intuitive and emotional desires. So, in the case of a goal to roll out a novel product, not only must you know that entering a new market will be good for the company financially, but you must also find yourself personally intrigued by the product's unique uses, for example. The resulting intention exists beyond the reach of calculative rationality and constant personal cost-benefit analysis. That does not mean it lies in a realm of irrationality or a lack of reflection. To make your intention personal, you must ask yourself a different set of questions.

Without a deep personal commitment to a task, you will simply wonder, "Who expects what from me? Will my boss appreciate my idea? How will I benefit? What are reasonable actions?" As a result, all that can develop, at best, is a superficial attachment to the task. You will be easily swayed when a better alternative comes up—or one that might impress your boss more—and you will always be open to the inevitable distractions of managerial life.[17]

Developing focus requires that you take time to consciously reflect, consider your alternatives, and ask, "Does it feel right? Do I really want it?" Those questions force you to reflect on what the goal or task means to you personally instead of allowing you to base your choice on potential rewards. Is it exciting? Is it something for which you can maintain your energy and commitment, even when facing adversity? Does it jibe with your personal values and beliefs? Can you stand behind it with head and heart?

Few managers are always automatically well focused. Most have to work at it, to face the dissonances between what they want and what they think is expected of them, and to deal with the anxiety that deep personal commitments create. Ultimately, focused managers must go through an act of inner consensus building in which they resolve their own conflicts and doubts.[18]

Let us see how one manager sharpened her focus by visualizing her intention and committing herself personally to that objective—and transformed herself into a more purposeful manager.

From Frenzied to Purposeful: Jessica Spungin's Story

At thirty-three, Jessica Spungin had just made associate principal at the London office of McKinsey & Company. Having started at the firm only five years before as an associate—as all business school graduates do—Spungin had risen in the ranks to engagement manager and then to associate principal, in essence, a junior partner.

But she already felt out of control. Consultants in her position typically take on more responsibilities of the partnership group and juggle multiple tasks and projects—all with an underlying expectation that they also be "inspirational team leaders." Shortly after Spungin's promotion in December 2000, new responsibilities piled up on to her already full plate.

"As one of my colleagues kept reminding me," she told us, "McKinsey is a cake-eating contest where the prize is more cake." She was asked to colead recruiting for U.K. universities and business schools, as well as to participate in an organizational research initiative looking at a data set of international companies that required lots of travel. In addition, she was senior coach for a team of six business analysts, responsible for monitoring their performance; providing professional guidance, coaching and feedback; and completing their evaluations. To top things off, she was asked to run an office party for 750 people, get involved in a training day, and help out on an organization project for a health-care company. By March 2001, Spungin was carrying the load of six different activities, all competing for her time.

Worst of all was the travel. Two clients had asked her to work on projects overseas, which meant commuting weekly between London, New York, and Tel Aviv. With all of her time focused on clients, her interaction with the internal teams—whom she had to lead and "inspire"—suffered. More often than not, e-mails and red-marked faxes replaced one-on-one coaching. "My teams would say, 'You sent us the most amazing e-mail feedback, but we would have preferred to discuss it with you face to face,'" she said. "And here I had been working overnight on the plane just to e-mail them feedback on time!"

Spungin knew that she needed to improve her effectiveness with her teams and somehow reclaim her schedule. But she faced another pressing issue: If she ever hoped to make partner, then she needed to specialize, building a professional program, which would demonstrate to existing partners that she had the intrinsic general qualities required at partner level as well as some distinct qualities that would be long-term assets to the firm. Finding a specialty meant that she had to spend her time on what mattered most to her professionally and to hope that those passions would all string together into a coherent story about her distinctiveness.

Spungin had two potential areas on which to focus: industrial clients or corporate banking. At London Business School she had studied organizational transformation. At McKinsey she had already worked on several projects for an industrial client in London, due to her functional knowledge of organization and leadership. She found the area challenging and intriguing—but felt that she had little experience there compared with her expertise in banking, gained from several years at Citicorp between undergraduate and graduate school. Unfortunately, banking excited her and challenged her less than working with industrial clients. Although Spungin had been straddling banking *and* industrial projects at McKinsey, she knew she could not continue that way, since the two areas just did not string well together. To make partner, she had to choose one.

Finding her area of distinction was a critical priority to Spungin. But she was equally worried about her performance as a team leader. The wake-up call came when she received her first round of formal upward feedback from her teams.

Sorting Through the Problem   Although Spungin had found the transition to managing people quite difficult at first, she had a reputation for being fun to work with and a very good people person, mentor, and coach—prized attributes within McKinsey's apprenticeship model.

So the first round of upward feedback she received as an associate principal (AP) surprised her—and the senior colleagues who reviewed her performance: It was extremely poor. The upshot? People preferred working with the other APs rather than Spungin. Sure, the teams found her effective enough when she sat down and spent time with them—but the problem was that she hardly ever did so. Team members also sensed that she was constantly stressed, and that had a ripple effect on everyone.

Clearly, Spungin had to make some serious changes. So when she began a training program designed to help senior managers sort through their personal and professional priorities, she did a lot of soul-searching and came to several realizations.

First, she admitted to herself that her poor team leadership stemmed from her own lack of confidence in her new position— something that, unconsciously, she had used her frenzied busyness to disguise. "They say consulting is full of insecure overachievers," Spungin told us, "and I was a classic example! I was always waiting for [my superiors] to find out my flaws. So when I found I was an AP . . . I never said no to people asking me to help out for fear they would think I could not cope. I never said no to a client who wanted me to be there for a meeting, regardless of the flying involved. I drew the boundaries based on what I thought was *expected* of me, not on the basis of what I was good at, or what I could physically handle."[19]

Second, and perhaps more important, Spungin admitted that, while she always had partnership as an unconscious goal, she never had the courage to really try to achieve it. Now she did, and she committed herself fully to becoming a partner at McKinsey.

"It was actually a very difficult goal to emotionally and intellectually commit to," Spungin said. "When you join McKinsey, you believe you will be asked to leave in two years—so, mentally you say, 'I am here for two years.' You never say, 'I want to be partner' because, chances are, you will not make it, and you want to avoid the heartbreak. Saying 'I want to be partner' is like saying to someone 'I love you'—it always makes you vulnerable."

Visualizing Outcomes—and Committing to Goals   Once Jessica Spungin became clear about her desire to be a partner, she could *visualize* herself as one and begin to think and see her life that way. And creating that mental picture allowed her to focus on the actions that would help her achieve her goal. One result was that she began to think in longer time blocks. Instead of planning, as she had always done, in three-to-six-month periods (essentially, from one evaluation point to the next), she began to think in terms of two to five years.

"When you start thinking in terms of a five-year time horizon," she said, "then you can prioritize. You cannot make things change in a few months. You need years to redefine yourself."

That simple shift in perception also led Spungin to take proactive steps toward *committing* to a specialty in the firm. Although she was one of the company's experts in corporate banking—and a focus in that area could provide her a clear path to partner—she realized that she did not feel passionate enough about it. She had already found herself enjoying her corporate banking clients less and less, and the thought of more of the same in the years ahead—working out end-game strategies, discussing outsourcing and joint venture options—filled her with dread.

The result? Spungin took a look at all of her projects and tasks through a new lens, asking herself, "How does each add to my personal and professional development—or not?" Her answers led her to stop working in wholesale banking, lecturing at conferences, and attending leadership group meetings in favor of zeroing in on what she felt most passionate about—organizational issues and the functional practice, an area in which she had already been working with several industrial clients.

This new focus on her own professional development also held the key to resolving her problems as a team leader. Not only did having a real direction improve her self-confidence; it also automatically pared down her schedule, leaving her larger blocks of time in which she could focus on her teams. To create even more time, Spungin started to phase her tasks in order of priority. Depending on the stage of events with each project, either an industrial client or another priority client would come to the forefront. She was very explicit with each client and each team about what she was going to do and what her priority at that moment was.

Ultimately, by choosing priorities, phasing projects, and refocusing, Spungin could devote more time to mentoring and coaching teams. As a result, her 2002 feedback review, exactly one year after she was rated second from the bottom in her peer group, rated her second from the top.

"I am now a lot more confident in my own ability to judge what I want to do and how much I want to do," she told us. "That came from having the guts to commit to McKinsey and say, 'I want to be a partner'; doing organization work rather than banking; changing the way I worked with my teams; and knowing when to take a breather once I had reached my physical limitations."

Jessica Spungin's story illustrates that focus is key for any manager who hopes to transform into a purposeful action-taker. And Klaus Karl's story demonstrates how a manager can reenergize himself—again, all with the goal of acting with more purpose. But a critical ingredient underpins both energy and focus: willpower. Harnessing willpower does not happen simply because an individual decides to engage it. A manager ignites her willpower only when she reaches a crucial phase in the process of undertaking a goal—what we call "crossing the Rubicon."

BOX 3-2

___

To Sharpen Your Focus . . .

Visualize the Intention.
   Ask yourself:

- What does my intention look like? What is a simple image I can keep in mind when I need to remember my intention?

- How can I accomplish my intention? What are the specific steps I will need to take to reach it?

Make a Personal Commitment.
   Ask yourself:

- Does this particular intention feel right? Do I really want it?

- Does my intention excite me? Is it something for which I can maintain my passion and commitment, even when obstacles crop up?

- Does my intention jibe with my personal values and beliefs? Can I stand behind it with head and heart?

___

FOUR

Moving Beyond Motivation
to Willpower

O N JANUARY 11, 49 B.C., Julius Caesar made a crucial
decision: to cross the river Rubicon with his army, thereby
effectively declaring civil war against Pompey, who held power in
Rome. With the words *alea iacta est* (the die is cast), Caesar resolved to return with his legions to the city. Once he crossed the
Rubicon and ventured into the Roman heartland, he knew there
was no turning back. Either he and his soldiers would take the
city, or Pompey would destroy them.

Caesar's decision changed the course of history. Before he
crossed the river, taking Rome had been merely an idea, a wishful
desire that he might achieve. After the crossing, it became an un-
alterable course, with the force of his whole will behind it—which
in itself practically ensured success.

To move from "motivation" to "willpower," a manager must
undergo precisely this decisive shift to total commitment. Managers who engage the power of their will typically have crossed
their own personal Rubicon. Indeed, the forces leading to that

crossing and those beyond it differ significantly.[1] Before it, a person experiences desire—the driving force behind often volatile and superficial motivation. At that time, a person can always go back.

Beyond that threshold, a person's knowledge and emotions fuse into the resolute intention that defines willpower. He stands firmly with head and heart behind what he wants to make happen. Action is persistent, almost obsessive, until the individual reaches his own "Rome." As he burns bridges behind him, his intention becomes clear. The only remaining question is, How to achieve it?

That force of will underpins what we identified as the two hallmarks of a purposeful manager: energy and focus. Willpower gave Klaus Karl the relentless energy to pursue his goals at SNI, and willpower drove Jessica Spungin's focus after she had committed herself to becoming a McKinsey partner. Willpower separates the executives who remain stuck in unproductive behavior from those who overcome their procrastination, detachment, or frenzied busyness to develop a strong bias for action.

Many managers have never witnessed, let alone experienced, willpower in action. Indeed, only 10 percent of the managers studied have felt fully engaged and driven toward a goal for which success is the only option. This chapter will illustrate how managers can cross the "river," marshal the incredible power of their will, and reach their own goals. Purposeful managers who create and leverage such willpower typically pass through four stages, each of which implies a specific step that any executive can take.

Before we look at those steps, let us explore more deeply the notions of motivation and willpower. Books on employee motivation abound, and motivational speakers remain in high demand. Yet, we see crucial differences between simply motivating people and allowing them to feel the power of their will in action.

Motivation Versus Willpower

We can trace the idea of willpower and its relationship to motivation back to an obscure academic debate that raged in Europe at the beginning of the last century. At that time, Germany was the center of academic research in the field of psychology—and two of its preeminent psychologists, Narziss Ach and Kurt Lewin, developed opposing theories about volition—what, for the purposes of this book, we have referred to as willpower.

Ach's careful research showed that, before a person's intention could become a deep, personal commitment, he had to cross a threshold of sorts.[2] Ach distinguished motivation, the state of desire before crossing this threshold, from volition, the state beyond it, when the individual converted the wish of motivation into the will of unwavering, resolute engagement. Lewin's field theory, on the other hand, denied that motivation and volition were distinct.[3]

Unfortunately, the Nazi party adapted the language of volition and will as its central philosophical tenant. The source was not Ach's careful experiments, but Arthur Schopenhauer's and Friedrich Nietzsche's ideas—distorted for the National Socialist cause—that posited the will as the original and primary force of all life.[4] Nevertheless, when the Third Reich fell, Ach's work on the concepts of volition and will fell with it.[5] Meanwhile, Lewin emigrated to the United States, where his leadership theories became famous. His influence is one reason why leadership training today so often focuses on motivation and managers continue to struggle with typical problems of volition, or willpower.[6]

The unfortunate Nazi co-optation of the concept of volition has long obscured one of Ach's important findings, which our opening story of Julius Caesar illustrates: the clear distinction between motivation and volition, or willpower. This unwavering commitment—the engagement of the human will—lies behind all dedicated and purposeful action-taking.

Note that the difference between motivation and willpower matters only when the particular challenge you face is difficult. Easy and familiar tasks do not engage the human will. Ambitious goals, long-term projects, high uncertainty, extreme opposition—such circumstances both need and stimulate the forces of volition.

For example, as Lufthansa went from near bankruptcy in the early 1990s to record profits in 1997, the purposeful managers whom we observed displayed just such a shift from motivation to willpower. Willpower enabled them to manage dramatic corporate changes. The engagement of their will empowered them to overcome barriers, learn from market setbacks, and persevere through the energy-demanding journey from a vision to its realization.

Motivation, on the other hand, is often triggered by external stimuli or the expectation of some reward. Yes, theoretical concepts as well as management practice acknowledge the role of intrinsic motivation—the internally driven desire to do something. But motivation remains in the volatile state of wishing to engage, feeling attracted by certain opportunities, or being tempted to act out certain behaviors. Ultimately, both intrinsic and extrinsic motivation are volatile because they are susceptible to changes from one's environment and from one's inner preferences. Since the expectation of some reward drives extrinsically motivated behavior, a more attractive opportunity could always come along or obstacles could appear that render the reward worthless.[7] Although intrinsically motivated managers enjoy their activities, enjoyment can always fade and desires can change.

Willpower goes a decisive step further. It implies the commitment that comes only from a deep personal attachment to a certain intention. Willpower springs from a conscious choice to make a concrete thing happen. This commitment to a certain end—not to just doing something but to achieving something—represents the engagement of the human will. Volitional managers are infected with an incurable need to produce certain results.[8] They are driven neither by the expectation of reward nor by the joy of carrying out particular activities. To the contrary, willpower enables managers to act in a disciplined way even in situations when they have no desire to act, feel unmotivated because they do not expect to enjoy the work, or feel tempted by alternative opportunities.

Take the case of Dan Andersson, a young manager who led Conoco's entry into the gas-station business in Finland. In an environment where a state-owned monopoly had controlled retail trade in the industry since 1947, Andersson's task was to establish both storing facilities and a network of Conoco service stations.

Breaking the power of the monopoly proved challenging indeed. Even though the market had legally been deregulated, the entrenched incumbent had a million tricks to hold on to its dominant market share. When Andersson tried to set up the first filling station, the incumbent lobbied against Conoco and its partners, and owners of neighboring real estate sites filed complaints, citing legal issues.

Andersson had his work cut out for him—but at some point early in the process, he had crossed his personal Rubicon, and he knew he was not going to give up. Part of what triggered that leap were memories of his own childhood in Finland—and the high prices and bad service that the gas monopoly had inflicted on the Finnish people.

"I pictured a movie called *The Untouchables*," Andersson told us, "and it completely changed my mood. It was about busting Al Capone in Chicago in the 1920s—and I felt we were doing exactly the same thing. We were busting the system. We were getting those unscrupulous competitors and conniving politicians and bureaucrats who were trying to use their dirty tricks on us. Actually, I ended up deriving huge energy from that unfairness." Conoco's successful retail business in that country today testifies to Andersson's "busting the system."

As Andersson demonstrated, motivation works from the outside in—with the environment defining what is possible or even desirable—and willpower works inside out. Inside is the will that defines the goal, the mission, the purpose. People with willpower decide what they want to accomplish and then work to modify the outside world, as needed, to achieve their goal.

How can you tell whether you have crossed the Rubicon? A move from motivation to willpower manifests itself in three ways.[9] First, it feels easy to begin taking action toward your objective. You know what you want, and you do not need further information or external stimuli to get started. Why? Because before making the crossing, you will have consciously considered and resolved your doubts and anxieties. You, therefore, do not suffer from the painful hesitation and doubt that motivation often implies.

You will also find that your perception is biased. All of your attention, energy, and preferences will focus on your intention, and you will constantly look for information that will help you realize it. Accordingly, you will block out contradictory information and will not feel distracted by routine disruptions—or tempted by alternative opportunities.

Finally, with willpower, you will respond in new ways to obstacles. Faced with negative feedback, lack of interest from (top) management, resistance from colleagues, or any of the other impediments to purposeful action-taking, motivation often dissipates. But willpower triggers the opposite response. Barriers will only make you redouble your effort and commitment. Abandoning your task will simply not feel like an option.

How, then, can managers learn to act with volition? What urges them to cross the Rubicon, and what keeps them on track once they have waded through the water? Our observations of the process of creating and leveraging willpower reveal some distinct stages through which purposeful managers pass.

Four Stages of Volitional Action

Julius Caesar's decision to cross the Rubicon ultimately led him to conquer Rome. At that moment he committed unconditionally to his intention, thereby engaging his will. We have identified three additional stages, however, that people pass through on their way to achieving a goal. The four total phases are as follows: forming your intention; committing unconditionally to your intention (crossing your Rubicon); protecting your intention; and finally, disengaging your intention.

Forming Your Intention

The first phase for reaching any objective is to decide on the intention or goal you hope to achieve. This is the point from

BOX 4-1

Are You Acting from Motivation or Volition?

Before Crossing the Rubicon . . .

- You are in a state of weighing options. You continually question whether your decision is the right one or ask yourself whether your chosen project is worth the effort.

- You have trouble getting started working toward your goal, and you have difficulties resuming work after interruptions.

- You cannot quite muster the energy consistently to move toward your objective.

- You lack a precise action plan, and you have only a fuzzy idea of your goal's result.

- Obstacles easily discourage or deflect you from your goal.

After Crossing the Rubicon . . .

- Your will defines your actions; you keep your intention in the forefront of your mind, continually seeking information that confirms your intention and will help you implement it.

- You easily take action toward your goal; you focus your energy and attention totally on your objective, and nothing distracts you.

- You have no doubts that you want to achieve your goal.

- You have a precise idea of the result you want to achieve—and how to get there.

- Obstacles in your path make you redouble your effort; failure is not an option.

which both Klaus Karl and Jessica Spungin had to begin: Before they could hope to direct energy toward an intention (in Karl's case) or begin to consciously focus on it (in Spungin's case), they had to pass through a period of seeking, exploring, and beginning to formulate an objective.

Often, an opportunity or challenge that attracts your attention and interest triggers such an intention. But the opportunity cannot be routine; you must see it as exciting, as something special that would really make a difference. Intentions that later become deep personal commitments will also inevitably tug at your emotions in some way. A purely cognitive framing of an intention never leads to volition. You must feel something in the challenge that demands and justifies "personal skin" in the game.

In the early phase of forming your intention, however, you may have only a vague idea of what you can do. Your attention will stray; your perceptions meander. But gradually a particular idea may gel, and your thoughts, perceptions, and emotions will solidify. The more precisely and vividly you visualize that intention, the better you will know whether you really want to pursue it.

For Swiss entrepreneur Wim Ouboter, the process of forming the intention that would eventually become his famous microscooter began one day in 1990 when he felt like eating a sausage.[10] He lived just outside of Zurich—too close to the sausage shop to use the car, he felt, or even to go to the trouble of getting the bike from the garage. But the distance was also too far to walk: It was a "microdistance," to use Ouboter's term. In a flash of inspiration, the then thirty-year-old banker sensed an opportunity—to develop a very small scooter as a vehicle for traveling such distances. There was a clear emotional link. His sister suffered from the physical disability of having one leg shorter than the other. To include her in their activities, his parents had encouraged the entire family to use scooters.

Enthusiastic about the idea and motivated to develop a business from it, Ouboter started building the first prototype of the microscooter. However, when he started using it publicly, the bemused looks of people embarrassed him. Even his friends dismissed his idea. Discouraged, he put the prototype in his garage and forgot about it for five years. Every now and then, he would use it, often secretly at night, and purely for fun. He had not yet built a strong personal commitment to his intention.

Committing Unconditionally to Your Intention

When you cross your Rubicon, your superficial attachment to your idea ends. You accept the challenge and essentially declare war. You commit unconditionally to your intention and cannot turn back.

Often this decision follows a gradual process—a series of events that awakens you somehow to the fact that you must choose one path or another. But sometimes a catalytic event triggers the choice. Just ask Wim Ouboter.

In 1996, five years after he abandoned his scooter in his garage, some neighborhood children found it. As Ouboter watched them enjoying his prototype, his enthusiasm returned: "Children really love something about this scooter," he thought. He began to think again about creating a business around it. But he knew he had to weigh the pros and cons carefully; leaving his occupation as a banker to start such a business was risky indeed.

Finally, his moment of commitment began when his wife challenged him to realize his dream. After he told her about his renewed excitement, she said, "If you think this [scooter] is a good idea, then make it happen. . . . You must decide: yes or no?" She added that if he decided *not* to do it, she never wanted to hear another word about it.

Ouboter struggled two more days with his decision, weighing his doubts about leaving his banking career against his excitement about the scooter. Finally, he could answer definitively: "Yes, I want to do it," he said. *Yes.* He had crossed over. He would do whatever he must to make the world love his little scooter.

Ouboter's experience illustrates one essential requirement for crossing the Rubicon: real choice.[11] Without choice—either in reality or in your perception—you can have no free will, no volition.[12] Making a real choice involves weighing options, becoming aware of the pros and cons of your intention versus alternative options. That means resolving all your doubts and conflicts, as Jessica Spungin did before committing fully to becoming a partner. Another essential requirement: You must recognize and accept personal responsibility for your goal, despite all logical excuses.

That responsibility begs one important question: Can you, as a manager, truly commit? Pause, reflect, and choose carefully. One manager told us, "I sleep on any important decision for at least one night. I need some distance from the idea and the context. . . . Sometimes interesting opportunities look and feel completely different at home. . . . If I decide to do something and I am still convinced the next morning, then I know that I am ready to commit."

Once you have reflected on your choices and leaped across the river, you enter territory in which you must guard your intention at all costs.

Protecting Your Intention

Companies full of frenzied or detached managers sap focus and energy from purposeful action. Like Odysseus, who bound himself to his ship's mast when he passed the alluring—but deadly—Sirens, as a volitional manager you must consciously protect your intentions against distraction.[13] How? First, by managing your environment; second, by controlling your thoughts, including those that inhibit your confidence; and, third, by maintaining positive energy.

Volitional managers find ways to *manipulate their environment* to stay the course. That might mean creating certain social pressures that increase the cost of abandoning your intentions, be it through publicly making commitments, consciously setting challenging deadlines for certain deliverables, or asking relevant stakeholders to monitor your activities regularly. Other ways to guard your intention include blocking out certain time periods that you devote exclusively to your project. Or you might try minimizing distractions by, for example, deciding to check e-mail at specific times during the day. Then, as you near your goal, you may want to deliberately increase your accountability by holding more review meetings, for example. Any one of those strategies will prevent you from losing either your energy or your focus on your goal.

You must also protect your intention by *controlling your thoughts*. When you begin to question your objective—as you inevitably will—you need tools to help you deliberately refocus. Try recalling the magical moment when you crossed your Rubicon: What promises did you make to yourself at the time? Volitional managers do not simply ask whether they are doing the right thing. They use a sequence of questions that help them visualize, first, what would happen if they failed to achieve their goal; second, how great it will feel when they succeed; and, third, the specific steps they will need to get to their final objective. By allowing yourself to visualize and experience that tension between the worst-case scenario and the best, you can likely resolve it and refocus on achieving your objective.

Controlling your thoughts includes maintaining your confidence in your ability to achieve your goal.[14] That is why volitional managers purposefully find ways to renew their belief in themselves. Such confidence will allow you to deal energetically with negative feedback and obstacles. If you feel overwhelmed or incompetent, you will lose your energy and give up on your goal more easily. Drawing on past positive experience can help you maintain courage and confidence. Try visualizing a former success, vividly and in specific detail. Recall especially the ways in which you overcame certain obstacles in your path—and then remember the feeling you had at the moment of victory. All of these strategies will help you protect your sense of competence on the road toward achieving your goal.

Finally, to protect your intention, you must find ways to *maintain positive energy*. Besides personal discipline and strength, positive energy is the most striking characteristic of volitional managers. Rarely pessimistic, they tend to have fun and enjoy their work. How? By managing their stress and creating healthy ways to experience their feelings.[15] For example, Klaus Karl learned to release tension and maintain energy by deliberately learning to "work hard and play hard." As a volitional manager, you must actively experience emotions that create energy. Remember that, over time, even the most exciting project can become boring or difficult. To protect your intentions, you must plan reenergizing events—some kind of reward for passing milestones, for example. You must also find ways to turn painful emotions into healthy energy. Conoco's Dan Andersson did precisely that, by converting his anger and frustration with the monopolist's dirty tricks into enthusiasm for "busting the system." Wim Ouboter did the same when he brought his idea of a microscooter to market.

In 1996, after the fateful conversation with his wife, Ouboter formed his company, Micro Mobility Systems, and soon began to develop a new prototype—a full six years after he had abandoned the scooter in his garage. Around that time, Micro Compact Car AG (MCC AG)—a joint venture between Mercedes-Benz and Swatch—introduced the "smart" car to the European market as a minivehicle that was easy to maneuver and park in tight city spaces. The company's marketing slogans—"Reduced to the maximum" and "The future of micro mobility"—caught Ouboter's eye, and he decided to approach the carmaker. He made his prototype just the kind of hip product that buyers of the smart car would appreciate: compact, foldable, and lightweight. The auto executives agreed to equip each smart car with a scooter in the trunk, provided that Ouboter could mass-produce them with sufficient quality and reliability. It seemed Ouboter was on his way.

With a target sales figure of 40,000 scooters, Ouboter found a reliable manufacturing partner in Taiwan. But by the time he returned from Asia, the managers of smart had changed their minds. Cancellation of the agreement felt like a punch in

Ouboter's stomach—yet it did not stop him. In fact, it only served to make him more determined. "I said, 'I will do it anyway,'" Ouboter told us. "I will show the world that this is a great thing."

Still believing in an overall market potential of 40,000 scooters, Ouboter started looking for other distribution channels, marketing programs, and entry strategies. Suddenly, a miracle happened. The scooter caught on in Japan, then in Europe, and then all over the world. By December 2000 Micro Mobility Systems was selling 80,000 microscooters *daily*, with revenues increasing at 1,400 percent per year. "Looking back, the smart cancellation was the best thing that happened to me," said Ouboter. Although painful, the setback energized him to maintain his positive energy and succeed against all odds. Ouboter also protected his intention by managing his environment. For example, he asked both his wife and his father to monitor his progress at specific milestones. He also made sure he controlled his thoughts. For example, whenever he began to doubt himself, he remembered that moment of disappointment when the people from smart car reneged—and the promise he made to himself. Or he would recall how he felt when he heard how the scooter had succeeded in Japan. All of those things helped protect his intention and spur him on toward his goal.

Disengaging from Your Intention

At some point, volition can also blind you, making disengagement extremely difficult and painful.[16] Two different types of problems can emerge: First, you might persist in action-taking even when a project is obviously unrealistic or doomed. You put more and more effort into achieving the impossible, instead of abandoning your intention and initiating new courses of action.

The second type of problem arises for opposite reasons: You fall so much in love with your project that you cannot disengage even after you have completed it. Instead of deactivating and moving to a new challenge, you find reasons to continue investing time and effort.

How do you protect yourself from this kind of volitional pathology? One way is by establishing "stopping rules" right from the beginning. Stopping rules are especially important for risky projects and actions where requirements for the outcome are unclear. You must define these rules for yourself—the particular critical events or intermediate results that should trigger your initiative's stopping point. By clearly defining the expected results, you will identify when to brake. Without such clarity, you may not recognize that a project is spinning out of control. In cases of multiphased, sequential intentions, effective deactivation rules are particularly important if you hope to stop investing in one phase and move to the next.

Wim Ouboter displayed just such an ability to channel his volitional energy into new projects when the time came. After the boom in the scooter market—beginning in 1999 in Japan—came the inevitable bust in 2001. For the first time in months, Ouboter stopped to reflect, and he realized that he had achieved more than he had ever dreamed he would. Dealing with the boomerang effects of a dead trend made him see that pouring effort and energy into trying to reactivate the earlier boom was a waste of time. Still convinced of his vision of micromobility, he started playing with new ideas. He developed prototypes for various microvehicles, contacted various firms, and produced a number of new product ideas, such as a microsnowboard, a one-foot skateboard as a lifestyle product for BMW, a trendy-looking trolley for IKEA made for carrying furniture home on public transportation, and another trolley for transporting equipment for the Swiss army.

Purposeful action-taking depends on engaging the power of the will. Not only does willpower galvanize your mental and emotional energy, it also enables you to make your intention happen against the most powerful odds: distractions, temptations to move in a different direction, self-doubt, and negativity. Willpower is the force that strengthens your energy and sharpens your focus throughout the action-taking process.

BOX 4-2

To Harness Your Willpower, You Must . . .

Form your intention. Find a goal that you hope to achieve. This idea should appeal to you emotionally in some way. At the beginning of the process, your intention may still be fuzzy or vague, but eventually you should have a concrete and tangible idea of what you want to make happen. You must visualize it.

Commit unconditionally to your intention. Make a conscious choice to put your whole focus and energy behind your objective. At that moment, you cross the Rubicon; often because of a series of events or one catalytic moment, you choose to take personal responsibility for making your intention happen. You resolve your conflicts and doubts around achieving your objective, and you become sure that you can stand behind it with your head and heart.

Protect your intention. First, take measures to control your environment to keep out distractions and maintain your focus. Second, control your thoughts—by using tools such as visualization—to keep your goal in sight and your confidence up. Third, maintain positive energy by managing painful emotions and finding ways to trigger positive emotions (again, visualization is key).

Disengage from your intention. To do this, you must have established from the outset what your stopping rules will be. For example, decide how you will recognize when you have met your goal—and, alternatively, how you will know when to redirect your energy if your goal becomes undesirable for some reason. Then commit to following those rules.

Yet willpower is something we rarely see among managers. Few managers have the courage to say a real yes to their intentions—which inevitably means saying no to other options. Few ever make a conscious choice to commit to their intentions unconditionally. When they do, they have crossed their personal Rubicon. In the following chapter, we will examine what, exactly, occurs at that crucial moment of commitment—and look at three strategies that will help you move from merely feeling motivated to actively engaging your willpower.

FIVE

Crossing the Rubicon

Rachel Davis, an analyst in a U.S.-based financial services company, just received a job offer for a position in the firm's Frankfurt office. Although she knew that the company wanted to expand its presence in Europe—and needed U.S.-trained analysts to break the big German banks' grip on the market—the offer surprised her. She was doing very well in her job and never considered working abroad. Success overseas could supercharge her career and expand her horizons, but she risked losing her visibility at the head office while grappling with a foreign land and a foreign language.

Davis had reached her personal Rubicon. To cross or not to cross? On this side lay the familiar; on the other, the unknown. Crossing to Europe could ultimately lead to failure, or it could make her career take off like a rocket. The Frankfurt office needed her answer: yes or no.

WHAT HAPPENS at the Rubicon? What defines that critical moment in which a person moves from a motivated state, waffling about intentions, to a volitional state, acting with willpower toward solid objectives? What would Rachel Davis need to cross over?

In this chapter, we explore what actually happens at that moment of decision: how to activate and harness the volition needed for purposeful action. The key, we found, is aligning your emotions with your thoughts about your goals.

The Defining Moment

When we asked managers about the moment at which they crossed their individual Rubicon, they recounted some common experiences. First, at these moments, they discovered their deepest, innermost feelings about their goals. Second, their thoughts about their goals assumed a new clarity, and they became confident of achieving their objectives. Third—and the most important element for triggering volitional action—*they aligned their emotions and thoughts about their goals.*

Managers find that their emotions often pull them in different directions. One moment, they feel good about making a certain thing happen, and then they begin to worry about the possible outcomes. Sometimes they were excited about their idea but also worried that they would not live up to their boss's or colleagues' expectations. Other managers in our study felt emotionally removed from their projects, even though they occasionally could muster a measure of excitement about them—for example, when they thought of the reward or recognition that might result.

Unlike mere thoughts, feelings tend to be all-encompassing: They embody an overall experiential assessment of a situation.[1] Mixed feelings and ambiguous emotions inevitably create stress and internal turmoil, and struggling with such emotional conflict can burden managers excessively.

The first step across the Rubicon, then, involves overcoming such emotional conflict. This often lengthy, painful process results in clear emotional focus—either a decided inner rejection of the undertaking, or unconditional emotional support in the form of enthusiasm and determination that spurs you on. Deep personal commitment and true grit replace emotional confusion.

The second step involves a similar resolution of uncertainties about goals or approaches to an objective, except that the resolution occurs on the level of thought rather than feeling. All managers juggle several goals simultaneously, and most face inner conflicts about prioritizing those goals, partly because they have only a vague idea of the desired results, and partly because they spend a lot of their time on what they consider to be useless activities.[2] The expectations of others or the demands of formal policies heavily influence them. Managers consider themselves caught between conflicting goals because seemingly pointless tasks absorb most of their time and energy.

Clearly, managers will always have conflicts about goals. Contradictions and the pursuit of multiple projects are inevitable in managerial jobs, and the tensions they create can even stimulate creativity and innovation. But when such conflicts become extreme and last for long periods, they sap energy, lead to halfhearted action and a counterproductive short-term orientation.[3] As with conflicting emotions, a lack of clarity about which goals to strive for becomes a personal burden. The result? Managers become overwhelmed by time constraints, dissipate their energy, and, ultimately, perform poorly.

With the crossing of the Rubicon, these conflicts about goals disappear. Confidence and determination regarding priorities replace confusion and inner doubts. Managers who have tuned out the white noise in the background find that their feet no longer drag.

The third feature of crossing the Rubicon—and the one that proves key for acting with willpower—is that emotions and thoughts about goals align.[4] Many managers, however, report a disconnect between their feelings and their rationally developed goals. Strong psychological conflicts and a sense of discomfort result, blocking purposeful action.[5]

At the Rubicon, managers resolve this dissonance. We observed that managers who crossed the barrier between motivation and willpower no longer perceived a contradiction between the things they felt were rational and the things their gut told them were right. Instead of acting purely from either emotional impulse or instrumental rationality, they stood behind their undertakings both emotionally and intellectually. This act of aligning emotional and rational forces strengthened and emboldened them to act persistently and purposefully.

How, exactly, can managers effect such alignment for themselves—and perform their jobs with a bias for action?

Aligning Your Thoughts with Your Emotions About Your Goals: Three Strategies and One Limitation

A manager's thoughts about her goals and her emotions about them usually spring from such different sources that aligning the two can challenge even a seasoned manager. But people can align their thoughts and emotions by relying on one or more of three strategies.[6]

The first strategy attempts to strengthen goals primarily through harnessing emotions that support those goals.[7] The second strategy is to manage emotional impulses that might hinder pursuit of those goals. Both of those strategies rely on some form of emotional self-discipline—you must either rein in negative tendencies or else outfox them.

FIGURE 5-1

Aligning Your Thoughts with Your Emotions About Your Goals

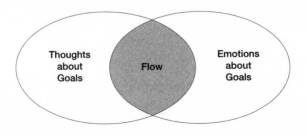

So, while those strategies are useful and even necessary at times, over time they can become self-defeating.[8] Managers who consistently marshal the full force of their willpower also adopt a third strategy: achieving the state of flow (see figure 5-1). In this state, a person's rational goals and emotions naturally overlap, or flow, concurrently.[9] Let us look now at each of the three strategies.

Strategy #1: Harnessing the Emotions That Support Your Goals

Managers who adopt this first strategy deliberately establish positive responses to strong emotions for their intention that keep them on track. Often, they rely on some specific visceral images.[10] Dan Andersson of Conoco used this volitional strategy while battling an oil and gas monopoly in Europe. By visualizing the characters in the movie *The Untouchables*, he could see himself as "busting the system"—an image that gave him the force to meet his objective in a very challenging situation.

To create such an image for yourself, go through the same steps described earlier to protect your intention:

- Imagine what would happen if you chose *not* to pursue your goal after all. Ask yourself how that might feel, and what others would think of you.

- Ask yourself, "How will I feel once I have met my goal? What will others say? And how will I feel later, long after I have achieved my objective?"

- Paint a mental picture of everything that you will have to do to achieve your desired result. Ask yourself, "What kind of energy would I need to achieve these goals? How will I deal with setbacks?"

By repeatedly playing with these kinds of images, you will focus your will on both the positive and negative aspects of the journey to achieving your intention—and soon reconcile the tension between them.

Why does this reconciliation matter? Because focusing on just the positive aspects of the potential outcome results in a certain superficiality of intention, while focusing on just the problems means that you rely only on difficult emotions—such as anxiety, shame, or guilt—as driving forces of your actions. This comparison of positive and negative aspects of the endeavor, combined with the act of envisioning the effort necessary to achieve it, allows you to marshal the excitement and commitment you will need to pursue your intention.

Strategy #2: Managing the Emotions That Distract You from Your Goal

Most managers have mixed feelings about an objective right from the start. This is particularly true for companies in trouble, where unpleasant tasks dominate most managers' work. In Lufthansa's transformation, for example, every manager faced painful tasks under difficult circumstances. Most of them experienced not only substantially increased workloads and long-term strain but also a very high level of emotional tension. The leader of one of the project teams told us, "This project pushed me to my limits. Apart from the crushing workload, what took so much effort was remaining persistent to overcome obstacles, solve all kinds of new problems, and deal with other people's emotions as well as my own."

Most managers respond to these intense emotions in two different but equally ineffective ways. Some seek escape. When confronted with fear or frustration, they quit pursuing their goals, either from insecurity or discouragement. In change situations or in challenging projects, they quickly confront their limitations and typically detach themselves as managers.

Other managers completely suppress their overwhelming emotions. To prove their strength, they deny their doubts too readily. While initially that strategy may work, the negative energy eventually catches up with them. The reality of the situation overwhelms them, and they typically switch to a higher-priority project—or so they tell themselves. Thus, many projects ultimately fail because managers begin work without confronting all their emotions about the goal.

To stop derailing yourself, you need active self-management of both negative and positive reactions. Some emotions feel so good that they tempt you toward a goal that conflicts with the intention on which you have already decided. To manage such distracting feelings, you could conjure up images that make such alternative options feel subjectively unattractive. Consider Peter Meyer, a young lawyer responsible for the building laws for a major urban entertainment center in Europe. Meyer loved his role in the ambitious, extremely challenging project. But a recent change in his firm's promotion policy diminished his chances to become a partner, and the center's investor had begun to question its potential profitability. Delays, long decision processes, and the lack of acknowledgment lessened Meyer's passion for his job. He started envisioning leaving the firm and launching his own business. Soon, the constant friction between his job dissatisfaction and his excitement about alternatives began to wear him down.

Meyer knew that he must manage these emotional distractions to keep himself on track. As he began to weigh his options, he soon realized that, in private practice, he would never work on what he loved—the big, challenging projects like this entertainment center, or airport privatization, or a variety of other large innovations. How much would he miss that kind of work? He realized how passionately he actually felt toward his current project. Meyer soon understood what these alternatives would mean for him: routine, mediocrity, boredom. He saw himself as a top lawyer in a powerful firm, not a soloist who accepted any mundane job to survive. Gradually, opening his own office lost its appeal. Meyer recalled these sentiments whenever he faced unsavory tasks during the urban entertainment center's development and when his doubts resurfaced. Because of his exceptional effort and success, his firm made an exception to its new promotion policy—by making Meyer a partner eight months later.

Apart from distracting emotions, however, you must actively manage the negative behavior that keeps you from pursuing your goal. Most important, you must acknowledge strong emotions—confront your doubts about your goal by visualizing the entire process toward achieving it. Then ask yourself, "What might happen that will frustrate, frighten, or bore me stiff?"

To unleash your willpower, you must do more than merely manage or eliminate problematic emotions: You must find ways to transform negativity into positive energy. Instead of letting obstacles weaken or discourage you, you must activate your pride and use the emotional consequences of failure (like shame or anger) to mobilize extra effort.[11] Tools—such as forming positive mental pictures, processing disturbing thoughts with a trusted person, or even just injecting humor into your outlook—will help transform your energy.[12]

For example, one manager of a change project at a high-tech firm found that a particular senior manager really worried him and his team. Fearing that this person would attack the team's best ideas, its members decided to role-play, acting out the worst-case scenario as a group. With one teammate's portrayal of the senior manager, the group was soon laughing and putting its worries into perspective. The upshot? Team members safely confronted their emotions and identified positive ways to behave when the time came to confront the objector. Everyone felt prepared and positive about the encounter.

Similarly, in the early product development stages, Wim Ouboter met with a potential partner who ultimately mocked the microscooter as something that "no kid would ever want to be seen riding." Ouboter leveraged that hurtful comment to make the scooter a reality, recalling it whenever he needed a boost.

Another way to transform negative energy is to distance yourself from the situation. For example, one Lufthansa manager involved in a highly demanding transformation project told us, "When I decided to manage the transformation, I was frightened of the immense responsibility. But just when the pressure became too high and I was on the brink of backing out, I started imagining the whole thing as a life-size adventure game. Suddenly, I was actually excited about becoming part of the process."

The Limits of Self-Discipline

Both Strategy #1 (harnessing emotions that support your goals) and Strategy #2 (managing emotions that distract you from those goals) require that you learn to outwit yourself. With these strategies, you build self-discipline and strength so that the rationality of your goal overrides the vicissitudes of powerful emotions. Particularly disciplined managers can muster energy for what does not initially excite them or even defies their intuition. They do so, as we have shown, by generating positive energy while dealing actively with their negative responses to strong emotions. So, rather than simply disciplining themselves to achieve an end, they acknowledge their worries and fears, while also thinking positively about their goals and how to meet them.

Sometimes these strategies for harnessing willpower can be limiting—especially when they involve leveraging emotions to create energy for action.[13] For example, we have met several managers who were very strict with themselves, constantly working against their personal inclinations and emotions. They readily committed themselves to other people's goals without considering their own needs. Then they imposed heavy self-discipline on themselves during implementation, thereby neglecting their own needs and emotions yet again. They continued pursuing these goals even when they felt no desire to do so, could no longer stand behind their actions, or even found themselves inwardly resisting those goals.

Their strength often became a weakness, however, when the gap between their goals and their individual needs persisted or widened. These managers quite naturally felt anger, anxiety, and guilt about the difference, and so, over time, their exaggerated self-discipline worked *against* achieving their objectives. Overly disciplined managers whom we observed became easily overwhelmed and ultimately failed. By constantly trying to meet others' expectations, they never developed their own standards to measure themselves and their achievements. Some constantly questioned their worth and appeared harried, in inner turmoil, and constantly afraid that they fell short. Unlike colleagues who could draw energy from their emotions, these individuals lacked the ability to act naturally. As a result, they tired more quickly and, over time, typically hit a wall. By denying their needs, they ended up feeling increasingly irritated and alienated. Instead of controlling their emotional responses selectively and investing those emotions in their tasks, these managers allowed suppressed emotions to turn against them. That kind of permanent tension between feelings and goals often led to burnout—and ultimately such disciplined managers lost sight of their objectives entirely.[14]

Clearly, then, managers should not overuse Strategies #1 and #2. Although suppressing inner needs can work in the short term, it can eventually cancel out or reverse any forward steps and is unsustainable. For sustainable, volitional action, managers should engage in intentions that include a large overlap of rational goals and deep emotional preferences—thereby entering into the state of flow.

Strategy #3: Achieving the State of Flow

Managers who continually act with volition do not merely harness certain emotions to support their goals or discipline themselves to manage emotional impulses. They also select a strategy that might seem timid at first but ultimately strengthens them. They search for solutions in which their thoughts and emotions about their goals naturally overlap, and, if necessary, they modify their goals to harmonize with their emotions. Achieving such a state of flow—a phenomenon first identified by psychologist Mihaly Csikszentmihalyi—requires greater courage and effort during the process of decision making.[15] In the long term, you will have more emotional energy for meeting your objectives in the flow state. Your willpower will be at full throttle because you will achieve even ambitious goals without perceiving your actions as strenuous. Rather, you will feel completely absorbed by your work.

The story of Wim Ouboter includes just such a moment of reaching the flow state. For a long time, Ouboter struggled with how he could continue his career in banking while also pursuing his dream of making the scooter business a reality. After a while, the idea overwhelmed him, and he abandoned the scooter idea altogether. When Ouboter caught himself daydreaming about his little scooter, he realized that he would have to build his entire career around it, rather than build it alongside a banking career. So he did. This act was not an impulse but a careful decision, based on conversations with his wife and much soul-searching. Eventually, he felt that starting the business was worth any risks involved. Both his head and his heart supported his decision, and, in this state of flow, he began to pursue his dream.

To act with willpower, then, you must expand and reinforce your flow area in many different ways.[16] You must first become aware of your emotions and your learned responses to them—which means identifying and understanding your deepest desires and, conversely, why you might be resisting your established intention. Freeing yourself of external expectations—such as by taking some time off work to think and reflect—can help you pinpoint your hidden emotions and honestly answer for yourself what course you wish to take. Once you are aware of your negative behaviors surrounding certain emotions, you must scrutinize those behaviors carefully. Again, apply visualization tools. Envision the various alternatives for taking action as precisely as possible, and then ask yourself how you truly feel about each option. Or picture the individual steps of your goal, watching for negative emotional responses that taint that picture.

By accompanying your assessment with a rational analysis of what causes those emotions, you will align your goals with your emotions. Why? Because considering your goals will keep you from making overgeneralized, superficial, or hasty decisions based on simply a gut feeling.[17] Try asking yourself, for example: "What do I really feel like achieving? What sort of activities trigger feelings of fear or frustration? Can I tolerate those feelings, or does intolerance hinder me?"

At this point you can use this assessment of your feelings selectively—to modify your goals if necessary. By reorienting your undertakings, redefining your goals, or striking out on new paths, you will address the emotional issues that might hinder you later—and you will enter fully into a state of flow.

BOX 5-1

Align Your Thoughts with Your Emotions About Your Goals

Triggering the certainty and determination you need to cross the Rubicon and commit unconditionally to your intentions means making sure you align your thoughts and emotions about your goals. Try the following strategies:

- *Strategy #1: Harnessing the Emotional Responses That Support Your Goal.* Deliberately create energizing responses to emotions around your intention. Visualize specific images to keep focused steadily on your goal. Ask yourself:

  - How will I feel if I do not achieve my goal?

  - How will I feel once I have succeeded?

  - What setbacks will I meet along the way, and how might I deal with them?

  - Which emotions automatically prompt me to act positively?

- *Strategy #2: Managing the Emotions That Distract You from Your Goal.*

  - Which emotions elicit distracting behavior that draws you away from your goal? Use imagery to make those behaviors subjectively unattractive.

- Acknowledge painful emotions, such as doubt and frustration, and talk about them rather than acting to avoid them.

- Transform negativity into positive energy. Use positive mental pictures; process negative thoughts with trusted friends and colleagues; inject humor around your fears; use other people's nay-saying to mobilize your pride and spur you toward your goal; distance yourself from negatively charged situations to decrease their power.

- *Strategy #3: Achieving the State of Flow.* Although the above two strategies can work in limited ways to help harness your willpower, only the flow state can sustain volitional action. To achieve that state, you must:

  - Strategically search for solutions in which goals and emotions naturally overlap. If necessary, modify your goals to harmonize with your emotions.

  - Identify and understand your deepest desires and, conversely, why you might be resisting your established intention. Try taking some time off to think and reflect—and pinpoint hidden emotions.

  - Scrutinize negative responses to emotions carefully. Picture the individual steps to take toward your goal, watching for any destructive reactions. Ask yourself, "What sort of activities, events, or exchanges trigger feelings that result in negative behavior? And, "Can I tolerate these intense feelings, or do they overwhelm me?"

Matthias Mölleney, the head of HR for the now defunct Swissair, vividly illustrates how an individual can align his thoughts and emotions about goals—and how our three strategies can help people leap from motivation to volition.

The Case of Matthias Mölleney

Swissair was in financial trouble even before September 11, 2001. The consequent closure of U.S. and Canadian airspace, however, along with flight diversions, cancellations, and plummeting demand resulted in huge losses and devalued assets at the airline. Within the month, Swissair decided to lay off as many as five thousand people across all layers of management.

On the last Sunday of September, CEO Mario Corti called Matthias Mölleney at home. "Meet me at the office," he said. Mölleney, an executive committee member in charge of human resources for Swissair, had been with the company only a few years. But he was a twenty-year industry veteran, knew his job well, and loved the airline business.

That night, Corti told Mölleney that Swissair had to signal to the outside world that it was downsizing quickly. One such signal: reducing the size of the executive committee by dropping several members, including Mölleney. Mölleney would keep his HR job but lose his committee status. He was devastated. How could Corti demote the one person who would look after the welfare of all those laid off? And what would that say to the already battered company and angry unions? How could company leaders fail to see that HR played its most critical role in such a crisis? "My thoughts and feelings just bounced around in my head like Ping-Pong balls," Mölleney told us. "My rational mind told me I should leave. It was clear that we would have to dismiss between three and five thousand employees. And if I did not have the CEO's full support, I knew I could forget being able to do the job properly. . . . I had always believed that my central responsibility was to the employees. But I could no longer see a way out."

Mölleney was completely torn. He had the option of leaving, but his original goals at Swissair kept coming to mind. Doing good human resource work—especially now—was critical for the company and important to him personally.

"This voice in my head was saying that, despite everything, I would grow into the new situation and I might even use some innovative measures to do a great job," Mölleney said. Despite the tough times ahead, he felt responsible for his people and could not abandon them. In fact, he felt truly needed. Still, the thought of taking on this new role filled him with negative energy. "I did not trust the company at all anymore," he said, "and I felt uncomfortable and completely paralyzed."

For three days, Mölleney felt locked in indecision, as if sealed in a bubble, completely unaware of his environment. Although people around him perceived his paralysis, he was engaging in an intense inner dialogue. Every time his head convinced himself to leave the company, his gut objected, and he could not decide either way.

The Moment of Resolve

The bubble broke when one of his most trusted people approached him. Both a subordinate and a well-wisher, she spoke candidly. She told him she could see that he was struggling over whether to leave the airline. "I see three possible scenarios," she said. "First, you go to another company; second, you stay but are mentally somewhere else; or third, you find your focus here again and build up the same energy level you had before, and we take this thing head-on together. None of us wants the second scenario to happen because it would increase the burden on us and the company. Please take this to heart. We really need you now." That day on his way home, Mölleney decided to stay. "My gut was telling me that if I did not try, then I would never be able to stand the sight of my own reflection," he said. "It would have been all too easy to leave, but I was ready to do anything to ensure humane dismissals and to deal with the crisis as well as possible. It was clear to me more than ever how much I—Matthias Mölleney—

was needed. I was ready to take on the risk and show everyone how important the human resource role is in this type of process."

What had happened? Mölleney had discovered what really mattered to him. Basically, he had modified his goals to align with his emotions, achieving a state of flow that would allow him to carry out the very difficult work ahead. Rationally, it would have been better to leave the company. But after his intense inner battle, he realized that his commitment to his people was so important that he adjusted his goals to his gut feelings, and he developed an agenda that made sense. Where he once saw calamity and restraint, he now saw opportunity. For example, he had initially assumed that he could never execute a mass layoff without his former decision-making powers. He now realized that the turbulent waters ahead would likely blow to bits the existing corporate hierarchy, creating a vacuum that any willing person could fill. He mitigated his doubt while reinforcing his conviction that this project was important. As a result, Mölleney garnered an unconditionally positive outlook: a sureness about what mattered most and the courage to undertake a difficult challenge. He knew that, in the end, he would pride himself in showing the corporate kingpins how vital, skilled human resource workers were in such a predicament.

"My presence was clearly guaranteed to make a positive contribution, and that was crucial," Mölleney said. "I had experience handling complicated and sensitive situations effectively. And I knew what was important for everyone—as few layoffs as possible . . . and then the creation of new jobs. That was my duty to the employees and the company. *That mattered*—not the limitations and stumbling blocks and lack of recognition from the executive management."

Maintaining the Flow

Although deciding was difficult, Mölleney no longer doubted his decision. Still, many people, including his family, could not comprehend his loyalty to Swissair, especially after a front-page story appeared in a national newspaper under the headline "Duds Ousted from Top Management." The story named and blamed the dismissed executive team members for Swissair's crisis. "This news was really hard," Mölleney told us. "My kids were being picked on at school. I was under an incredible amount of pressure, but I took time to explain to them why I had to stay."

At some point, however, he simply resolved to shut out others' expectations, including his family's, and listened inward. On October 2, 2001, the Tuesday following Mölleney's decision to stay, Swissair was grounded. The sudden bankruptcy shocked employees and managers alike because no one believed that this national icon would be left to die. Yet, the entire fleet was on the ground in a matter of days.

Mölleney, too, was shocked. He heard the news on the radio while driving to the office. When he arrived, he was greeted by an overwhelming silence: no one bustling about; no airplanes flying above.

"Seeing so many huge, red-and-white airplanes on the ground and everything so still was really frightening," Mölleney told us. "The fleet grounded. No more money for fuel. You have no idea what this meant for Switzerland, for the Swissair employees, and, therefore, also for me." Mölleney's resolve, however, was untouchable. He was in the flow of achieving his objectives: He thought, "This is going to be tougher than anything you have ever done before. But you will do it—no matter what happens."

Soon after, Corti, with the executive board's support, dismantled the management team and reduced the overall corporate organization from four hundred people to thirty. Mölleney was one of the few who stayed through the wind-down. Swissair would relinquish most of its flight operations to its regional airline subsidiary, Crossair. The challenge was to keep Swissair in operation during the winter season so that Crossair had time to prepare for assuming the intercontinental routes. Mölleney strove to keep Swissair's work force motivated and productive. Had the employees gone on strike or slipped on safety during this period, the Crossair takeover would have failed.

Layoffs continued. After a while, the executive management consisted solely of the CEO. Mölleney knew that eventually he would have to write his own notice and dismiss himself from the company. To the bafflement of friends, former colleagues, and family, he remained committed. He had already accustomed himself to the idea that this period would be extremely difficult and would require his ingenuity and acceptance of unusual operating conditions.

The downfall of Swissair became front-page news in Switzerland and beyond. Hundreds of journalists arrived. Feeling betrayed by the banks and the government, CEO Mario Corti was unavailable for comment, and so the media focused on Matthias Mölleney. The people issues came to the forefront in this situation, both as a focus for the media and as a natural result of the closing of the airline, and he became the key person in charge of the whole process. During this time, Mölleney had many discussions with Corti—who thanked Mölleney for all his hard work. Corti also openly acknowledged that his decision to demote Mölleney earlier had been a mistake.

By March 2002, most of the goals had been achieved. Crossair had taken over the remaining Swissair operations, and a new airline, Swiss, formed. Mölleney's role in the process ended. As he watched the Swissair logo being removed from headquarters and the planes, Mölleney reflected on the total experience: "Our work was done here. Emotionally, I struggled to leave the airline world that I loved so much. But two things helped me cope: first, all the positive feedback from so many Swissair employees and, second, the knowledge that I did everything that I could possibly have done. I have never regretted my decision to endure the tragic death of Swissair."

————

Clearly, crossing the Rubicon and engaging your willpower—as Matthias Mölleney did when he acted with such integrity during the demise of Swissair—requires an investment of time and energy. More than anything else, it requires that your thoughts and emotions about your objectives align. Managers who never create such alignment find that their doubts continually resurface and that the process of achieving their goals ultimately exhausts them. But managers who do can unconditionally engage their will: They act with confidence and persevere against all odds.

This chapter focused on how individuals can manage their inner emotions to act purposefully. But many sources of nonaction often lie in managers' working environments. In the following chapter, we will examine how managers can deal with such traps and maintain their energy and focus.

SIX

Overcoming the Three Traps of Nonaction

Jack Lippman was chief operating officer for a $150 million electronics components manufacturer based just outside of Philadelphia. Although he worked twelve-hour days, he often thought that he was just spinning his wheels. He always lacked time for thinking through the long-range issues that the firm needed to consider to survive in a downwardly spiraling market. He struggled to keep up with the immediate demands of his job, which overwhelmed him. Not only was he in charge of manufacturing and logistics, but he also kept track of the sales and marketing operations. Even if he had time to develop a plan for tackling big-picture issues, the company's resources were limited right now. How could he hope to funnel money into a new strategic operations project—streamlining the supply chain to minimize customer inventory—when his CEO was considering layoffs? Lippman felt he had few choices indeed—and his job felt like *one endless to-do list that never seemed to get him, or the company, anywhere.*

I N THIS CHAPTER we return to the topic of nonaction. What are the causes of the kind of nonaction that Lippman suffered in his job as COO—and what could he do to overcome them? While the problems with engaging willpower relate to a manager's inner conflicts, in this chapter we will examine those traps associated with a manager's environment. In other words, how can managers like Lippman overcome their belief that their jobs do not allow purposeful action? Lippman's case illustrates three traps of nonaction that we have commonly found among managers who get stuck on the riverbank, seemingly unable to leap with a bias for action.[1]

The first is the trap of *overwhelming demands*. Many managers are caught up in webs of expectations that completely overwhelm them. Their day-to-day jobs are so absorbing that they have difficulties reflecting on their goals, asking themselves what really matters and making sure that they make certain things happen. As a result they do not take willful action but remain busy with active nonaction—doing many things that actually do not make a significant difference.

The second is the trap of *unbearable constraints*. Many managers feel squeezed in narrow corsets of rules, regulations, or budget restrictions and believe that they have no space for autonomous action. They feel discouraged by corporate constraints to pursue goals that they consider significant.[2]

The third trap of nonaction is *unexplored choices*. Focused on the demands and constraints of their jobs, most managers develop tunnel vision and concentrate on immediate needs and requirements. They do not perceive or exploit their freedom to make choices about what they would do and how they would do it.

Typically, a manager can overcome many but not all the constraints to working with a bias for action. In the preceeding paragraphs we sketched out the traps of nonaction. Most of them can be overcome. However, there are constraints and limitations that actually prevent purposeful action.

All managers who overcome the traps of nonaction actively manage their jobs and working environments (including the traps of nonaction). But we have observed one critical quality that all purposeful action-takers share: None of them operated within the bounds of their prescribed job descriptions. Managers who exercised their will took responsibility for their freedom to decide and take action. They actively influenced their working contexts as well as their tasks. How? They either reshaped their jobs—reducing demands and constraints while expanding their choices—or they changed their own perception of their obligations, limitations, and freedom to act. In some cases, however, the only alternative was to change their jobs, as Thomas Sattelberger did when he left his previous employer—where the gap between his vision and top management's priorities would have made it impossible to create a corporate university—to join Lufthansa. In our observations, such cases are relatively rare. In most instances, managers can influence demands, constraints, and choices to create space for purposeful action within their existing jobs.

Let us now examine each of the three traps in turn.

The Trap of Overwhelming Demands

The basic raw materials for building commitment for your intention are attractive opportunities. Managers who get caught in the trap of overwhelming demands become prisoners of routines. They do not have time to notice opportunities. Their habituated work prevents them from taking the first necessary step toward harnessing willpower: developing the capacity to dream an idea into existence and transforming it into a concrete intention.

Most cases of overwhelming demands stem not from managers' actual work situations but from how they deal with those situations.[3] How do you know whether there's a problem with the way you approach your job?[4] For one, you deem some aspects of your work important, but you can never find time for them. Or you might feel under constant pressure. The most dangerous of all is believing that you are indispensable.

Managers who fall into the trap of overwhelming demands typically do so because they fail to actively influence those demands. These managers take demands for granted and simply respond to them, rarely questioning whether they actually make sense or whether one could reshape them. Feeling always "under the gun," these managers never find time to ask themselves, "Am I busy with the right things?"

The simple fact is that being busy is easier than not. Most managers cannot admit that a fragmented day is actually the laziest day, the day that requires the least mental discipline and the most nervous energy. Responding to each new request, chasing an answer to the latest question, and complaining about overwhelming demands are easier than setting priorities.

Fortunately, most managers can overcome their habitual fire fighting.[5] To do so, however, they must first clear the most difficult hurdle: the belief that they are indispensable. Managers who complain about having too little time often thrive on the sense of importance that their busyness generates. They enjoy being at the center of frantic activity where people continually ask them for help, information, or advice. If they were honest, then they would really not want more time—especially time to reflect![6]

Purposeful action-takers deal very differently with demands than their busy colleagues do. Rather than simply responding to any request that gets thrown at them, they manage their demands by

- developing an explicit personal agenda,
- practicing slow management,
- structuring contact time, and
- shaping demands and managing expectations.

Develop an Explicit Personal Agenda

To minimize the constraint of overwhelming demands, you first must develop a clear personal agenda.[7] That means coming up with a precise idea of what you want to achieve in your job. For example, rather than keeping general aims in mind such as "growth" or "good customer service," try crafting a vivid mental representation of your objectives that includes ways to achieve them.[8]

Take the case of Lufthansa's Thomas Sattelberger, whose dream was to create the first corporate university in Germany. Although he had multiple demands on his time at Lufthansa, he also had a detailed vision of his goal that enabled him to distinguish important tasks from unimportant busywork. His image? A temple with three pillars—one for each stream of development measures he hoped to build. The roof that bound the pillars together was a robust and visible institution—the Lufthansa School of Business. Supporting the entire temple—the foundation that was needed to build the corporate university—were proper operational HR processes.

The problem was that, as Sattelberger described it, the demands of his job during his first two years at Lufthansa left him struggling to simply build the foundation. "I thought that I would enter an intact HR department and would have wonderful conditions to start building the pillars of the temple that would become the corporate university," he said. "What I actually found was a complete mess."

Lufthansa's operational HR processes were in bad shape indeed. Small things, such as typing errors in contracts and a six-month response time to employee queries, took him two years to clean up. But he knew he had to improve the efficiency of HR processes because they composed the foundation of his temple. At the same time, he was developing the concepts and building the networks he would need for future steps in the process.

"Sometimes I felt guilty when I blocked about half a day every month for work on the corporate university," he recalls. "But I needed the time to make myself believe that my agenda was still valid, and that I was not being drowned in the operational HR work—although it occupied me more than 99 percent of time."

While reacting to demands can be distracting, the kind of personal agenda that Sattelberger created produces an opposite effect: It allows you to integrate the diverse, loosely related goals for your short- and long-term responsibilities into one broad master plan. You can, therefore, relate immediate and short-term priorities with their long-term purpose—which is ultimately much more inspiring than merely responding to demands.

Practice Slow Management: Reduce, Prioritize, and Organize Demands

All managers have to deal with formal procedures and ritualistic requirements to some extent—such as attending specific committee meetings and participating in certain events or functions.[9] But many demands that you might accept as given are actually discretionary in nature. You may, therefore, perceive more demands than there are, rather than recognize that some of them are really a choice.

Purposeful management, by contrast, means that you examine what you choose to do or not do. That way, you create space for tasks that are important, instead of doing what you like or find most familiar or easy. You will also not feel as tempted to jump impulsively from one thing to another.[10] Set priorities among your tasks, aligning your activities with your agenda. As one manager told us: "To achieve speed in the work that matters, one must practice slow management."

Referring to the chaotic situation he faced in his first two years at Lufthansa, Sattelberger told us, "Given this flood of activities, it was essential for me to have a clear idea of where I wanted to go. I had to structure my tasks and goals." He decided first to devote a certain amount of time to establishing efficient HR processes—installing a control system that monitored the quality, time, and cost for every important transactional HR process. The result? Clearly defined priorities based on each task's urgency and significance.

Structure Contact Time

Managerial work is primarily interactive and interdependent in nature; rarely do managers work on their own. The problem is that interacting with people is not only time consuming but also exhausting and the main source of the multiple interruptions about which managers often complain.[11] A typical trap of nonaction—which leads to feeling as if demands are overwhelming—is getting caught up in intensive interaction with lots of people.

Most managers spend much more time with their direct reports than is really necessary or even useful. Younger managers, in particular, often want others to consider them a good boss who cares about subordinates by being unrestrictedly available.[12] But keeping your door always open prevents you from accomplishing anything worthwhile.

How can you deal with this trap? Try structuring your contact time. For example, Sattelberger set the following policy: His door would be open at certain times, when anyone in the department could bring him problems that required immediate attention. That policy led not only to larger chunks of uninterrupted time but also to a higher quality of interaction with his people.

Shape Demands; Manage Expectations

Some managers constantly worry whether they are meeting others' expectations. Trying to please everybody, these managers tend to get absorbed in speculations about what others expect, about the best strategy to meet those expectations, and the consequences of not meeting them. Ultimately, the managers fail, not only because they find no time to pursue their own agenda, but also because in trying to please everyone, they typically end up pleasing no one.

Managing with purpose means realizing that you cannot meet everyone's expectations. Rather, you must concentrate on your key stakeholders. That means learning that saying a real yes and committing to something inevitably implies saying no to other things. It also means becoming aware of how much influence various stakeholders have on your ability to achieve your goals—and tailoring your responses to those individuals accordingly.

Purposeful managers differ from those who try to please everyone by not simply reacting to expectations, but by actively shaping them. Rather than merely meeting the expectations of your key stakeholders, then, you must do everything possible to exceed them. As one manager at Conoco told us: "Meeting expectations, accomplishing demands would mean absolute mediocrity for me. I must do better than what they expect. I cannot be creative if I only concentrate on doing what I have to do."

Another strategy is to present your own goals and ideas *before* your stakeholders have a chance to present their demands. But do so in a way that anticipates others' expectations—as well as provides a means to your own goals. That is just what Sattelberger did when it came to the demands of Lufthansa's management. He knew that, by exceeding his job requirements, he could move on to the next step of achieving his real dream. "I cleaned the pigpen," he recalls. "Nobody anticipated that I would cope with these draining issues. They were obviously surprised, and that was the moment for me to suggest new standards and new ideas. I wanted to transform the HR role and transfer it to a level that was higher than what they had ever imagined. It was a true innovation because no other company in Germany had such comprehensive business-driven HR processes." Had he instead tried to present his ideas before doing the dirty work—and gaining management's appreciation—no one would have accepted his ideas. As it was, Sattelberger's bosses began to see and treat him as the expert and believed in his commitment to create something really special. "I demonstrated to them that I would develop a means to support their business strategy, developing corporate entrepreneurship in a former state-owned company and maintaining change momentum after the crisis had eased off," Sattelberger said. "I addressed their concerns and showed them how we could jointly create new ways of solving their problems."

Shaping others' expectations is a long-term strategy that relies on developing sustainable relationships. While most managers do not consciously build and influence relationships, purposeful managers spend a lot of time developing their personal networks.

Rather than arbitrarily forming relationships with many people, then, try deliberately focusing your time and energy on developing strong and close ties with people who can influence the achievement of your goal.[13] While such an approach to building relationships might seem calculating, it never works without a component of genuine warmth, respect, and friendship. As a purposeful manager, use your social skills to weave your stakeholders into your agenda—and in the process jointly create new opportunities for purposeful action.

Besides overwhelming demands, some managers also feel they have too little freedom to act. Let us look now at the second trap that get executives into trouble: the seemingly unbearable constraints that so often lead to nonaction.

The Trap of Unbearable Constraints

Sometimes managers exaggerate the extent to which others' attitudes limit their opportunities to take initiative and make things happen.[14] They worry about what others will accept or tolerate, or they overemphasize the need to adhere strictly to procedures and policies. Others complain about resource restrictions, blind to how they can escape their routines. Focusing on their limitations and what they can't do, they essentially ignore what they actually can do.

One network manager in a large telecommunications company, for example, told us: "Already my day-to-day job drives me and my people to our limits. I have asked for additional resources, but we are in a difficult period. For a long time I have been wanting to introduce a quality control system to help us reduce errors. But given the situation, I do not see how I could get the resources to do that—or how I could do anything more than what I am currently doing."

Usually, constraints like those are real. But rarely are they as absolute as managers make them out to be. To unshackle themselves from this trap, purposeful action-takers adopt strategies like these:

- Mapping relevant constraints
- Accepting trade-offs

- Selectively breaking rules
- Tolerating conflicts and ambiguity

Map Relevant Constraints

The first strategy is to develop a clear map of relevant constraints; that way, you can systematically think through how to overcome them. Instead of lamenting about limitations, identify precisely which constraints hinder your ability to achieve your objectives. By doing so, you can more clearly picture the problems and resulting limitations. Most likely, you will discover that some constraints really do not affect your pursuits, and you can then focus on overcoming the key ones.

Thomas Sattelberger identified two critical constraints for building his HR temple at Lufthansa: a shortage of financial resources and a general lack of understanding in senior management regarding the strategic role that HR could play in the company's vision and purpose. He then focused all his energies on overcoming those two hurdles. So, rather than arguing for his vision as a whole—which would have frightened most of the stakeholders—he "introduced his temple stone by stone so that every single step was comprehensible," he told us. "Slowly and incrementally I created trust and belief in my argument about how HR development and eventually the university could play a vital role in supporting the corporate strategy. Over time they started seeing the whole picture."

Shortage of resources was the other critical constraint. In 1996 Lufthansa launched a strategic cost-saving program—Programm 15—which implied that departments had to save 4 percent of their total operating costs every year until 2001.[15] Investing in new projects was not on the agenda, and Sattelberger worked hard to overcome that resource constraint. Instead of cutting back on his initiatives, he agreed with the corporate controller who was responsible for Programm 15: Sattelberger could increase income by renting out Lufthansa's existing training center. But that was not enough to generate the half-million deutsche marks ($225,000 U.S.) he needed for proceeding with the initiative that he saw as central to his goal: the Explorer 21 program. The program that Sattelberger envisioned would involve about 210 participants who, in the course of one year, would work together with middle and top-level managers to create innovative projects and build Lufthansa's future.[16] To create the program, he needed CEO Jürgen Weber's support.

"It was not an easy conversation," Sattelberger recalled. "I explained that Explorer 21 was a key step toward business-driven HR development, and that Programm 15 would kill it. I argued with everything I had. I talked about the consequences if I did not get the resources to move on with this initiative." He and Weber then had several conversations with the controller and other top executives. "It was a huge step at the time—no other company in Europe had ever tried such a comprehensive development initiative," explained Sattelberger. "In the end Jürgen Weber said, 'For God's sake do it, but do it right and stick to your budget.' "

We have seen again and again how purposeful managers like Sattelberger reduce constraints and deliberately broaden their freedom to act. Some concentrate on influencing the attitudes of relevant stakeholders to obtain their support. Typically, they generate the required resources by winning one top-level sponsor. At the same time, they also build a broader network of relationships with various people to access resources such as money, information, advice, or competencies.

Accept Trade-offs

Sometimes, no matter how hard or persistent your effort, you cannot overcome all constraints. Most managers respond to these untenable constraints in one of two ways.[17] Some just give up when they cannot get exactly what they want and feel hurt and frustrated by the process. Others keep trying again and again, essentially repeating the same arguments endlessly—and ultimately banging their heads against the wall without making any progress.[18]

Purposeful managers deal much more flexibly with constraints. While never losing sight of their overall purpose, they tend to accept trade-offs more willingly than other, less effective managers. For every intention, you must separate the must-haves from the nice-to-haves. The more distinction, the more you will likely accept compromises where you can—and the more intensely you will probably fight for your must-haves.

Sattelberger coped with many setbacks and accepted multiple delays and even cancellations of different aspects of his initiative. He put aside his vision for the first two years to "clean the pigpen," as he put it. And he worked hard to increase earnings to get the green light for developing his cost-intensive learning networks. But all the while, he never allowed the basic vision to wither.

"Of course not everything worked in the first go," Sattelberger said. "But I never made compromises about some central things. I knew that not having a network culture was a major impediment for achieving the true potential of Lufthansa. Yes, cost reduction was important, but that alone would not make Lufthansa a great company. Explorer 21 was absolutely necessary for rebuilding the company's identity, for strengthening its ability to build and manage strategic partnerships, and for maintaining the change momentum." He, therefore, concentrated his main arguments on those issues—while still acknowledging to his superiors the need to save costs. Ultimately, he convinced everyone of his idea both by accepting trade-offs on questions that mattered relatively less for his goal and by demonstrating why Lufthansa needed to seriously invest in building its long-term strategic future.

Selectively Break Rules

Most managers we have observed tend to adhere to rules, procedures, and directions. They accept formal regulations as given and define their activities around those regulations. The result?

Usually, they simply react to changes of rules and objectives. Particularly in companies that lack stable policies, strategies, and directions, this rule following often leads to extreme short-term management behavior.

Purposeful managers take a more active stance when it comes to formal regulations. Not only do they question standing rules that they deem outdated or inappropriate, but they also break or circumvent the rules when it's absolutely necessary for achieving their goals. One sales manager at Conoco told us, "A number of regulations are absurd. If I would have followed them, I would not have achieved half of what I have. It is a tightrope walk—you have to be loyal to the company and not get into guerrilla warfare. But as I once read somewhere, 'Sometimes it is better to say sorry than to ask for permission.' I pretty much live by this principle. Nobody ever thanks you for following the rules—but they do thank you for doing a fantastic job."[19]

In most organizations, the informal, unwritten regulations create the biggest barriers to purposeful action.[20] Being explicit and limited to certain concrete issues and topics, formal rules are often less restrictive than the informal ones. Informal rules developed through cultural norms, habits, and shared expectations cover all areas of behavior and tend to be implicit and not subject to open discussions. As a result, they often shape and constrain individual action more pervasively.

Unfortunately, most companies' informal rules tacitly celebrate busyness—which is perhaps the most dangerous impediment to purposeful action that we have observed.[21] New projects are begun with great optimism but then seem never completed, or completed with minimal success. Rather than saying no when overloaded, managers in such frenzied cultures accept project after project that, in the end, they really cannot handle.

A bureaucratic culture and culture of strict top-down command and control similarly limits the scope of individual initiative. At the same time, a strong consensus orientation and team culture often equally debilitate exercising willpower.

More than breaking formal rules, purposeful managers succeed by challenging the restrictions that arise out of cultural
norms. One way you can do this is to break the code of silent ad-
herence by making these rules explicit and exposing them for open
debate. Entrenched dogmas survive only as long as they remain
unquestioned. As a purposeful manager, try unshackling yourself
from dogmatic restrictions by making them visible and, therefore,
untenable.

That is exactly what Andy Weston-Webb, the vice president of
human foods at Masterfoods Europe (or MFE, the new name for
Mars Inc.'s snack, pet food, and human foods businesses) did to
turn around not only the fortunes of his business, but also the
overall strategy of the $16 billion company. Early on, Weston-
Webb found that one of his biggest stumbling blocks was the company's own core philosophy—"We are in it for the long term."
That often translated into a tolerance for not turning a profit in
the short term; as long as product ideas were good enough, the
philosophy implied, profits would always come eventually. As a
result, there was a proliferation of new products often in categories unrelated to MFE's core competencies, and the business in
Europe had experienced zero overall growth over a ten-year period, incurring significant losses in several product areas.

Weston-Webb challenged this well-entrenched norm by carrying out detailed financial and market analyses, showing that in
the foods business, companies made money only when they had
a number-one or number-two position in the market and that
small-share, loss-making products outside a company's core categories rarely became profitable, high-growth positions over time.
With the data, he could confront MFE's and Mars's top management and gradually get them to accept his proposal for exiting
some businesses, containing others, and focusing his resources on
the core Uncle Ben rice and Dolmio sauce brands. The result? In
one year, Weston-Webb pushed the business up to 5 percent
growth, while simultaneously improving operating margins by
20 percent.

Tolerate Conflicts and Ambiguity

Most managers try to avoid conflicts and disagreement, opting for diplomacy and changing or suppressing their opinion. As a result, they waste time on strategies for navigating around potential conflicts and confrontations. But such superficial harmony carries a big cost: These managers do not feel the legitimate freedom to act; rather, their own insecurity constrains them. Purposeful managers, in contrast, embrace conflicts. The best of them disagree but do not become disagreeable, and all prefer the authenticity of open debate over the conspiracy of silent disharmony.

Sattelberger had several serious arguments with the Lufthansa controllers. He appreciated their focus on cost reduction but believed that it could become counterproductive. Although interested in building stable and good relationships with colleagues, Sattelberger had no compunctions about engaging in direct confrontation when progress on his vision was in danger. Sometimes he provoked conflicts to get attention for his agenda at top-management level. "There was one incident where the conflict with the controller was so intense that we had to discuss the issue with Jürgen Weber," Sattelberger said. "And I told him frankly that, given the limitations, all I could do was to excel in meanness and mediocrity. That was neither my purpose, nor would it help Lufthansa become the world-class organization that Weber wanted it to become." In the end, Weber completely agreed—and that never would have occurred had Sattelberger not fought for new standards and been willing to engage in difficult conversations.

Willingness to engage in conflicts to protect and pursue a deserving goal also requires an ability to live with ambiguity. In organizations of any size and complexity, conflicts—particularly those on important issues—rarely get resolved instantaneously. Typically, a process of escalation precedes a period of uncertainty, and as a purposeful manager, you must sustain your commitment through those periods. Sattelberger described, "There is a limit to how far and how quickly you can push. Eagerness beyond this limit is counterproductive. People get pissed off. You have to grit your teeth and carry on, even though at these times you are not certain which way the decision will go."

Ultimately, you can minimize the constraints you face by analyzing them realistically, confronting conflicts when needed, making trade-offs when you have to, and giving yourself an extra degree of freedom: that of tolerating ambiguity and learning to wait for the right time when the tide will turn.

Apart from constraints and demands, one final trap awaits managers who hope to act with purpose: the belief that they have few choices.

The Trap of Unexplored Choices

Choice is a prerequisite for engaging willpower. Yet many managers deeply believe that what they must do and how they must do it largely depends on the work context: the company structure, formal and informal rules, bosses' preferences and idiosyncrasies, resource constraints, and so on. They see little room for choice and, hence, few opportunities for autonomous, self-initiated, goal-oriented action.

As we have discussed, managerial jobs are indeed subject to both demands and constraints. At the same time, managers have much discretion over what goals they choose and the means for pursuing those goals.[22] Often managers do not recognize this freedom because they have fallen victim to the trap of unexplored choices. They fail to recognize their choices, and if they do see options, they do not exploit those options.

Purposeful action-takers, in contrast, avoid this trap by being aware of their choices; by expanding their opportunities and their freedom to take action on the choices they have; by developing personal competencies that both create choice and enhance their ability to make things happen; and by learning to enjoy both the freedom and the responsibility that choice brings with it.

Become Aware of Choices

Managers often develop a loyalty to and identification with their companies that amounts to psychological dependence. Programmed to serve the company's goals and strategies, they develop a tight inner contract: As long as they show their appreciation, obedience, and loyalty, the organization will take care of them.[23] As a result, they see few choices about what they can do in their jobs, and little need for choices. While these managers behave modestly and follow direction, they are rarely capable of taking the kind of purposeful action that we observed, for example, at the Hilti Group, based in Lichtenstein—the producer of high-quality tools for the building and construction industry.

The Hilti Group has spent twenty years developing managers who take responsibility for themselves and their goals. These managers feel that they have a choice—both in where they work and in what they do. In the words of Michael Hilti, former CEO and now chairman of the supervisory board: "I am glad that our people get calls from headhunters. First, I feel flattered that our managers are so attractive to other companies. But more importantly, I know and our managers know that they continue to choose to be with Hilti. . . . If they had no choices . . . they would always feel imprisoned."[24]

Another example: In Lufthansa's turnaround at the beginning of the 1990s, we observed that the most committed managers did not feel forced to stay but knew that, if they wanted to, they could leave the company and find a different employer. Peter Gerber, a manager responsible for wage agreements during the turnaround who's now head of Lufthansa's sustainable cost-saving program D-Check, told us, "This turnaround was brutal. After the gravity became obvious, everybody was shocked, uncertain, and anxious. At the beginning I was worried too. But then I realized that my destiny did not depend on the company. I am well trained, I have experience in different industries, and I will always find a job. Realizing that I had the choice not to be here gave me the courage to stay, to say, 'Yes, I want to engage in saving Lufthansa.' "

Choice lies at the heart of free will.[25] The actual exercise of choice is less important than the perception that you do, indeed, have a choice, even if you decide not to make use of your alternatives. How can you create that perception for yourself? Choices are not always obvious or tangible; you have to analyze and understand them. Most important, ask yourself what you perceive that you *cannot* do in your job. And then ask, "Who forbids me from doing that? What would happen if I did it anyway?"

Once you realize that you do have choices, you next need to generate specific alternatives for yourself.

Expand Your Choices

How do you expand your own notion of the alternatives you have for taking autonomous action? Try asking yourself, "What would it actually take to achieve my goal? Is there really no alternative other than the one I think that the organization is allowing me?" Dan Andersson of Conoco asked himself just those questions when he was trying to open a Conoco storage facility and distribution network in a long-monopolized market. He had a plan in mind—but he also made sure that, at any given point, he also had three alternative plans he could enact in case the first plan did not work.

Another way of expanding your sense of your alternatives and opportunities is by generating ideas through conversations and interactions with others. Managers without a strategic agenda of their own carry out their tasks and limit their conversations to their day-to-day work problems. As a willful manager, by contrast, you must seize upon opportunities to discuss your vision and ideas with different people inside and outside the company. By keeping your goals in the forefront of your mind, you will continually explore the perspectives of others and generate new choices for realizing your dreams. Although these conversations will not always help achieve your goal in the end, they will invariably lead to new insights and fresh opportunities.

You can also expand your sense of choice by seeking clarity about exactly what kinds of freedoms your job comprises. That means analyzing your job and working environment in a conscious way—including talking with relevant stakeholders about these choices. Many managers avoid such open discussions with their bosses. Some simply do not know how to address the issue of choice. Others shy away from raising these questions because they do not want to seem pushy. Often they feel insecure about their performance and lack the self-confidence to ask about their decision-making powers or about the degree of freedom they have to use their resources.

As a volitional manager, however, you must engage superiors in candid discussions about the scope of your job.[26] You will likely find that this kind of conversation will actually expand your space for action and increase your choices. Why? Because typically, bosses and other relevant stakeholders tend to see a job as bigger, and as providing more opportunities for innovation, than the manager herself might. Such a conversation will also help your bosses understand the constraints that their behaviors and decisions inflict on subordinates' ability to take action—and will give them the chance to make adjustments accordingly.

By using this strategy, you will actively involve your boss or other relevant stakeholder in your goals, giving them an opportunity to help you overcome any constraints. This is what Andersson did to overcome a potentially fatal flaw in his proposed solution. The only piece of land available for building the new Conoco facility was severely contaminated. By involving the local officials, the landowner, and a variety of other people in his agenda, Andersson found an ingenious way for Conoco to take over the land without assuming any historical liability. It was a highly creative solution that no one in Conoco could have generated without the participation of these external stakeholders.

Build Personal Knowledge and Competencies

Another way that you can expand the domain of your choices is by relentlessly building your knowledge and broadening and deepening your personal competencies.[27] Try investing both in a set of general skills as well as in a deepened knowledge and competence in one specific field of expertise. The combination of increased general skills and expert knowledge will help you generate and exploit choices in several different ways.

For one thing, greater knowledge and competence helps you identify choices more effectively.[28] A deep understanding of the company and its businesses, for example, is often a prerequisite for seeing the opportunities for self-generated and autonomous action. Especially important is the understanding of the invisibles—informal rules and norms, interpersonal relationships, and historically developed social dynamics—that influence how an organization receives and acts upon ideas.[29]

Such an understanding of the company also will help you perceive the positions of key stakeholders. Managers narrowly focused on only their own jobs often do not understand the concerns and biases of others and, therefore, cannot empathize. That means they cannot present their ideas in a way that aligns with the perspectives of those whose support would help implement those ideas. As you become known for your knowledge and competence, you will also gain greater freedom for action because of the credibility you will enjoy in the organization. Not only will your opinions receive more weight; you will also draw more opportunities to yourself, simply because people will seek you out for advice and collaboration.

But beyond lending you greater credibility, such competence will help you present proposals for your objectives more effectively. Broad knowledge of the organization, together with specific areas of expertise, allows you to marshal facts and arguments more persuasively. You will also improve your sense of timing, intuitively understanding when the moment is ripe to pitch your ideas.

For Sattelberger, those small windows of opportunity proved crucial for his success. "There are many little decisions and moments that simply do not count," he said. "But there are others that really make a difference. I had a good feeling for these decisive moments and concentrated my energy and attention on them. Not only were these my most important opportunities, but they also served as a precedence for the entire process. Winning these battles catalyzed the whole process."

After Sattelberger's continuous investments in shaping the pillars of his temple, the final step of putting on the roof—which was the actual construction and opening of the corporate university—became almost effortless. "The construction had taken place, and the building was ready," he said. "And then, in March 1998, I heard that Daimler-Benz was about to found a corporate university in May. And I said that I will not allow them to steal our show. I wrote a brief memo for the upcoming board meeting that proposed that the Lufthansa School of Business open its doors by April 1, 1998." Even though the board had not discussed the issue of an opening date so soon, there was no debate. After four years of work developing HR processes and energizing the change processes, "this formal step was nothing. We founded the first corporate university in Germany in April 1998, nine years after I had started pursuing my *idée fixe*."

So, managers who have developed both general and specific competencies feel more confident in actually using their power of choice.[30] Many managers hesitate to exercise choices, even when they are aware of them. Without the requisite sense of competence, they feel anxious and overwhelmed by the responsibility and the risk that inevitably comes with autonomous action. Often they fail to take initiative because they feel insecure about their decisions, do not trust their judgment, and feel that they need direction or backing for exercising their choices.[31] In contrast, managers who believe that they have the necessary knowledge feel more confident when dealing with unforeseen incidents or difficult tasks and find it easier to make decisions.

Enjoy the Freedom to Act

In the end perhaps the attribute that most decisively differentiates managers who see and act upon their choices and those who do not is simply the fact that they, quite literally, enjoy exercising choice and freedom to act. That usually means that managers must first recognize their freedom and become aware of their choices.

In Lufthansa's initial transformation phase, for example, we saw clearly the difference between managers who enjoyed having choices and those who did not. Although the work environment for everyone was extremely chaotic and unstructured, executives who enjoyed acting freely extended the scope of their jobs, expanded their choices, and pursued highly ambitious goals. As one action-taking manager told us: "I felt I had escaped from a classic organization where all that mattered were status symbols, hierarchy, and order—and had landed suddenly in a garage. I immediately felt comfortable. I was in a space where I could decide to do something and then roll up my sleeves and do it."

By contrast, the Lufthansa managers who did not enjoy this newfound freedom—who preferred to have clearly defined goals, concrete expectations, and close monitoring of their actions—reacted to the perceived lack of structure by becoming disoriented and paralyzed. Without constraints and clearly defined demands, without rules and stable processes, they felt extremely uncomfortable. They actually felt less able to make decisions and saw fewer opportunities to initiate action. One of these managers told us, "Somehow the entire process was diffuse and there was no transparency. . . . You could not make any plans. Long-term goals were clearly inappropriate and even in the short term, you felt unable to influence anything." The lack of predictability and structure, together with insecurity about requirements and roles, made this manager feel much more constrained than when Lufthansa was mired in bureaucratic controls. For him and several other managers we observed, the vagueness when it came to choice made them feel anxious, stressed, and threatened.[32]

Ultimately, the ability to see and exploit choices is a very personal matter. Some managers enjoy choice and derive energy and willpower from that pleasure—which, in turn, helps them overcome all the traps of nonaction (see table 6-1). Fortunately, enjoying the freedom to act is something that one can learn—by simply acting on that freedom. Thomas Sattelberger did. Why could he pursue his dream of the corporate university so relentlessly? As he told us: "I like to make things happen. And I am not too proud to roll up my sleeves and do the operational dirty jobs along the way. Having a vision and making decisions is fantastic.

TABLE 6-1

Overcoming the Traps of Nonaction

The Trap of Overwhelming Demands	The Trap of Unbearable Constraints	The Trap of Unexplored Choices
• Develop an explicit personal agenda	• Map relevant constraints	• Become aware of your choices
• Practice slow management: Reduce, prioritize, and organize demands	• Accept trade-offs	• Expand your choices
• Structure contact time	• Selectively break rules	• Build personal knowledge and competencies
• Shape demands; manage expectations	• Tolerate conflicts and ambiguity	• Enjoy the freedom to act

But the real joy and satisfaction comes with persistence, with doing hard and risky work."

What distinguishes managers who take willful action from those who do not has less to do with their working context than with their abilities to see the opportunities in those environments. That is what Joseph Schumpeter, the Austrian economist who gave us the theory of creative destruction, implied when he asked: "What differentiates the entrepreneur from others? Most people go about their normal, daily business and have sufficient to do thereby. . . . A minority with a sharper intelligence and a suppler imagination, see numerous new combinations. . . . It is a still smaller minority that acts. . . . The new combinations will always be there; the truly indispensable and decisive will always be the deed and the energy of the entrepreneur."[33]

As we have said, most managerial jobs tacitly encourage mindless busyness rather than purposeful action. No wonder, then, that managers so often fall into the traps of overwhelming demands, unbearable constraints, and unexplored choices. Fortunately, managers can overcome these traps, as well as other reasons for active nonaction that we have described thus far in this book.

We have outlined in this first part of the book how a manager becomes a purposeful action-taker: by developing energy and focus, building the resolve of willpower, aligning emotions with goals, and, finally, overcoming the traps of nonaction. Becoming a purposeful action-taker is not only important for the sake of a manager's individual effectiveness. It is also decisive for his capacity to lead others. Without energy, managers cannot motivate or inspire others. Without a clear focus on priorities, managers cannot provide orientation, channel other people's energy toward critical business issues, and set the right agenda for their company. The first task of managers it to take charge of their own capacity for acting with willpower. A second set of tasks, then, involves fostering willpower in others. This is a true leadership task that implies building the structural context, nurturing a volitional culture, and personally encouraging managers to make things happen that go beyond mere routine. Let us now turn to part II, where we will explore how to create the kinds of organizations that encourage and reflect such a bias for action.

Part Two

Cultivating a Company
of Action-Takers

SEVEN

Developing Purposeful Managers

The Organization's Responsibility

M ANAGERS MUST BE DOERS.[1] The first part of this book focused precisely on this personal action-taking dimension of the managerial job. Yet managers cannot achieve their goals in a vacuum; that is why companies and markets exist. In this second part, we turn to the leadership role of all managers: not to motivate others into doing (as many managers believe), but to facilitate others' purposeful action-taking.

How can leaders instill willpower in others and ultimately create organizations that consistently demonstrate a bias for action? Once they have transformed themselves into purposeful doers, they must craft a context within the organization itself that supports purposeful action-taking. Leaders can do this by undertaking two main tasks. One is to overcome the challenges inherent in building an organization of managers with a bias for action. The other is to weave the values of volition and personal responsibility into the cultural fabric of the company itself. Two organizations that we studied—British Petroleum (BP) and Hilti Group—demonstrate those tasks of the purposeful leader.

Let us look first at the challenges of creating a context that facilitates volitional action, and how leaders of BP overcame those challenges to save the oil company from collapse in the 1990s.

Building an Organization of Purposeful Managers

As we illustrated in part I, people engage their willpower only when they think that they have personal control over their situations. They must believe that they have discretion in terms of, for example, decisions on their work goals, content, and processes. They must perceive a sense of autonomy, of being able to choose and decide, of being in charge. Essentially, they must have a sense of personal ownership of their specific work domain.[2]

But creating such a context presents several contradictory requirements for the leader who wishes to build an organization in which purposeful action-taking can flourish. First, how can she ensure that the autonomous actions of any one manager will align with the overall goals and direction of the company? Second, how can she prevent one manager's exercise of willpower from limiting other managers' similar self-initiated action? Finally, how can she reconcile individual managers' need for the support of others in achieving their goals with those other people's need to exercise a certain freedom of choice?

The first question, of course, is moot in the traditional command-and-control organization, where the exercise of hierarchical dictation keeps corporate goals and individuals' tasks closely in sync. As we have seen, this very top-down deployment of goals has severely deprived modern corporations of the power and energy that human willpower can produce. But what of the opposite problem—when, through the exercise of personal choice, an individual's intention either splits from or directly conflicts with the company's goals and direction?

To benefit from volitional action that aligns with corporate goals, leaders must ensure that people at every level internalize the overall purpose of the company. The organization's goals must also become each individual's personal purpose. That means crafting a shared vision and a set of common values that everyone authentically subscribes to—not as an externally imposed constraint, but as a personal source of identity and meaning. To build a context for volitional action, then, purposeful leaders must develop in their people a shared commitment to an overall direction as well as to a set of common values and mutually agreed-upon norms of behavior. But what of the price of such volitional action? What of accountability? That brings us to the second challenge of crafting a context in which managers can work with a bias for action: How can a leader ensure that the freedom of one does not constrain the freedom of all? For example, if a manager chooses to pursue a goal of achieving the lowest cost that directly contradicts another manager's goal of achieving the fastest delivery time—the organization must somehow protect the freedom of both.

Clearly, individual freedom must have boundaries. Leaders must build organizations in which they set boundaries around the domains of initiative—for example, decreeing that one manager's will to build the business in France can coexist with another's freedom to build the same in China. But delineation by jurisdiction alone is insufficient. If the actions of one manager severely damage the brand in France, then managers in China will ultimately feel the effects—no matter who decreed what. So, the boundaries must also encompass those vital few areas of interdependence that extend beyond geography, product, and function.

Finally, since organizations exist because individuals cannot always achieve their goals all by themselves, teamwork—sharing of information, resources, and effort—becomes critical. Moreover, people must also feel emotionally supported within the organization. Which brings us to the third challenge: How can a leader reconcile individual managers' need for the support of others with those other people's need to exercise their own freedom of choice?

While the requirements of autonomy and support are straightforward, the challenge of effectively developing them lies in the tensions that exist across them. At the extreme, personal freedom and shared support are difficult to combine: Highly autonomous managers focus only on their own goals and tasks and tend not to share knowledge or resources with others, or to invest their own time and energy in helping others succeed. Supporting others often calls for some level of sacrifice in terms of pursuing one's own goals to the limit. Yet, to be effective, a company with a bias for action must find ways to make voluntary teamwork coexist with individual autonomy. For example, leaders can institutionalize the importance of peer relationships by ensuring that managers regularly receive 360-degree feedback, which, of course, includes peer evaluations. Or they can do what 3M does: designate a certain amount of free time each week for managers both to pursue personal initiatives and to support others in their ideas.

We have briefly outlined here how leaders can address each of the challenges of crafting a context for purposeful management. The real lessons in facing such challenges, however, become obvious when we see how an actual company handled them in practice. Let us examine now how one organization—BP, the United Kingdom's largest industrial enterprise and one of the three most powerful companies in the oil industry—granted its managers autonomy with boundaries, and practical and emotional organizational support, to create an environment in which purposeful management flourished.[3]

BOX 7-1

The Challenges of Building a Context for Purposeful Management

- How to ensure that the autonomous actions of any one manager will align with the company's overall goals and direction?

  ☞ • Purposeful leaders develop in their people a shared commitment to an overall direction as well as to a set of common values and mutually agreed-upon norms of behavior.

- How to prevent one manager's exercise of volitional action from limiting other managers' similar self-initiated action?

  ☞ • Purposeful leaders build organizations in which they set boundaries around domains of initiative, keeping in mind those areas of interdependence that extend beyond geography, product, and function.

- How to reconcile individual managers' need for the support of others in achieving their goals with those other people's needs to exercise a certain freedom of choice?

  ☞ • Purposeful leaders institutionalize certain norms and practices that allow voluntary teamwork to coexist with individual autonomy.

The Transformation of British Petroleum

In June 1992 BP was spiraling downward financially after a series of pivotal events: the transition from public- to private-sector ownership, which had coincided with the stock market collapse in 1987; the fall in oil prices after the Gulf War; and rising debts and increasing unit costs. On June 25 the board had to cut its dividends and fire its chief executive, Robert Horton.

Just a decade later, in 2002, the company was leading the restructuring of the oil industry, had reduced costs and debt, and was earning after-tax income of more than $1 billion a month. With annual revenues of $120 billion, BP employed one hundred thousand people in more than a hundred countries, becoming one of the three superpowers in the oil industry. Moreover, CEO John Browne—the chief architect of the renewed organization—won the title "Britain's most admired CEO" an unprecedented four times in a row. Many considered the company at the leading edge on a variety of issues from environmental protection and corporate governance to performance management and organizational design.

How did BP become such a model of both financial performance and corporate social responsibility? Two simple principles at the heart of the transformational changes at BP also provide a template for overcoming the challenges inherent in building an organization of purposeful action-takers:

1. *Space*: The first principle is that people need their own space—a clearly defined domain of activities that uniquely belongs to each individual—because only within such space can people's ability to take self-initiated and purposeful action come into full force. Yet, a necessary set of boundaries defined by the company's strategic and operating foundations—its vision, values, and beliefs—limits an individual's space.

2. *Support*: The second principle is that the main benefits of organizational scale and diversity lie in the company's

ability to support individual action—professionally and emotionally.[4] Professional support includes ensuring that managers have a reliable network of experienced individuals in the organization who will share their knowledge and support the process of volitional action. The emotional component of support directly facilitates a person's ability to deal with personal requirements of the job—for example, coping with stress or negative feelings as well as building up positive emotions such as courage, pride, or enthusiasm.[5] Again, such support comes from close personal networks that often consist of peers but can also include mentors and colleagues off-site. Leaders, of course, offer a combination of both emotional and professional support: They act as role models and provide inspiration, intellectual stimulation, and backing when someone questions an individual manager's decisions or actions.[6]

Creating the Space for Volitional Action   John Browne has a simple belief: that people work better in smaller units because the closer they can identify with objectives and targets, the better things happen. Therefore, the best way to achieve excellent overall performance is to divide up the big long-term targets of the company into small units that can take full ownership of those targets.

Browne tested this belief when he was Chief Executive of Sohio, BP's North American subsidiary. He restructured an operation that had chronic losses into a separate unit; installed managers who represented the "normal" talent levels available to the company (to ensure that the outcome was not purely a result of outstanding local leadership); and gave those managers complete autonomy to run the operation, freed from the company's traditional central controls. The unit's dramatic performance improvement became a key lesson for Browne by the time he took the reigns of BP in 1996.

As the corporate CEO, Browne restructured the company into 150 business units and yielded to the unit managers a great deal of freedom to run their operations autonomously. As an essential corollary to this concept of space for volitional action, BP has created a performance-contracting process designed to provide a clear line of sight between the performance of individual business unit leaders and the corporate-level business goals. The contract, defined annually and reviewed each quarter, specifies a few financial goals—profit before tax, cash flow, investment, return on capital employed—and a few high-level nonfinancial targets. "Once the contract is agreed upon, the unit leaders are completely free to achieve the goals in any way they want, with no interference from anyone outside that unit," said Rodney Chase, BP's deputy CEO. "At the same time, it is a promise they must fulfill, and they know that." Everyone takes targets very seriously; failure to meet them usually means a transfer for the manager.

British Petroleum has also crafted a statement of overall direction and a manual of core policies that both define the boundaries of the space and align individuals' self-initiated actions with the company's overall purpose. In the words of Rodney Chase again: "Space is not limitless; there are the boundaries. These club rules are not negotiable. If you want to join the club and enjoy the excitement of running your own business with freedom and autonomy, then these are the rules of the club that you must obey."

In defining these boundaries, top-level BP leaders have articulated, with precision, both the company's economic goals and its role in society. The economic dimension is simple. As Chase put it: "We are in the business of exploration, production, refining, and marketing of oil and gas and some closely related chemicals. Everyone in the company must be clear about that—no one should be thinking of making money by selling music, real estate, or whatever. We are not in those businesses."

While this domain definition helps managers shape their own goals, the company's four-part commitment to establishing itself as a force for good influences the means for achieving those goals. The first part is personal safety. BP is an oil company, and employees face considerable safety risks. British Petroleum takes that responsibility to heart. "When you invite people to work for you," Browne says, "you should send them home in the same shape as when they arrived. That is a minimum requirement for respect of a person, and you must take that terribly seriously." The second part involves behaving responsibly toward the environment. "There should be no damage done to the environment as a result of our operations," Browne says. The third is to be fair and antidiscriminatory. "It does not matter what you stand for in terms of your race, gender, sexual orientation, or religious beliefs," says Browne. "All that matters is merit." The fourth part involves giving back to and investing in the community from which employees come, to "narrow the gap between life within the company and life outside the company." A brief policy manual summarizes the practical implications of this four-part commitment that all employees promise to follow.

Building Support Networks   At the heart of the support structure in BP lie fifteen peer groups. Each peer group consists of a network of related business units within a particular business stream—essentially those in similar businesses, facing similar challenges. For example, all the large, mature gas fields are in one peer group; all the marketing heads in Europe are in one peer group; the business units responsible for new projects are in one peer group; and so on.

Initially, BP's use of peer groups focused on a process called Peer Assist. Business unit leaders regularly provided help to one another within their peer group—to help identify the best strategy, to learn more about a new area of work, or to validate a decision in the form of advice or actual resources through a Peer Assist. For example, Polly Flinn, a former Amoco executive who was posted as BP's retail business unit (BU) head in Poland—asked for assistance from four BU leaders in her peer group. They came together in a Peer Assist team to look at the Poland strategy and give Flinn their advice. After Flinn—a relative newcomer to the retail business—implemented the advice from the Peer Assist, performance of the business turned around from a loss of $20 million in 1999 to a profit of $6 million in 2000. "This was BP at its best," said Flinn. "I and my team in Poland obtained strategic and operational insight from the most respected experts in BP. At the same time, it was also a developmental opportunity for those who helped us."

Once BP institutionalized the Peer Assist process, it extended the use of peer groups to a process called Peer Challenge, where the power of the peer groups drives the company's performance management and resource allocation processes. Peer Challenge requires that all business unit leaders get their plans, including investment plans, approved by their peers, before finalizing the performance contract with top management. Polly Flinn said, "It is all about convincing people in similar positions to support your investment proposal, knowing that they could invest the same capital elsewhere, and going eyeball-to-eyeball with them—and then having to reaffirm whether you have made it or not over the coming months and quarters."

In an added twist, BP has extended the peer process even further—the three top performing business units in a peer group are now responsible for improving the performance of the bottom three. According to Rodney Chase, with Peer Assist and Peer Challenge, "what we have raised to an art form is that if I have a good idea, my first responsibility is to share it with my peers, and if I am performing poorly, I will get the peer group to help me."

While the peer groups are the primary mechanism in BP for providing both professional and emotional support to managers, inspiration and activating leadership is provided by systematically emphasizing the coaching and mentoring requirements in senior management roles. This leadership responsibility goes deep into the BP organization: The group vice presidents are responsible for coaching and mentoring the business unit heads, and so on. At senior levels, support is also provided by a set of expert external consultants who work one-on-one with individual executives on an ongoing basis.

The Positive Cycle of Purposeful Action   Clearly, BP has managed to overcome the three challenges of building an organization of purposeful managers. First, BP's leaders ensure that the autonomous actions of managers align with the company's goals by establishing the economic targets as well as the human and social club rules themselves. Second, its leaders rely on the peer group process to prevent one manager's exercise of willpower from limiting other managers' similar self-initiated action. Finally, BP leaders leverage that same peer group process to ensure that business unit leaders can draw on the professional and emotional support of their colleagues needed to pursue their goals.

So far, we have presented the story of BP as a snapshot; a static picture of how the features of individual autonomy, organizational alignment, and mutual support are actually achieved in a company. What this description misses is the vital dynamics of BP's organization, the symbiotic process in which its definition of space and support have, over time, mutually reinforced each other to create a positive cycle of purposeful action.

As the combination of space and support facilitated managers' purposeful action-taking, BP's business performance started improving. This improvement led to two outcomes. First, top-level managers—including Browne, Chase, and others—developed growing confidence in their strategy of delegating authority to the business unit leaders, thus further reinforcing those leaders' sense of empowerment and personal control.[7] Second, the company found greater resources to invest in developing the support infrastructure, including IT systems, and in building the conversation and communications mechanisms. Those investments, in turn, further strengthened the mechanisms and processes of Peer Assist and Peer Challenge.

As this symbiotic effect of space and support evolved, a culture of active collaboration gradually emerged. Rodney Chase described this process of culture change: "In our personal lives—as fathers, mothers, brothers, or sisters—we know how much we like to help someone close to us to succeed. Why did we not believe that the same can happen in our business lives? That is the breakthrough, and you get there when people take enormous pride in helping their colleagues to succeed." As this culture evolved, it led to two interrelated but separate outcomes. First, managers' self-confidence grew. As they set themselves tough but achievable targets and achieved those targets through their own initiatives and peer support, they developed the confidence to set slightly tougher targets. In that process, they strengthened their sense of autonomy and their volitional capacity. Second, the culture also led to the reinforcement of mutual trust and friendship, which strengthened the peer group processes of professional and emotional support.

The net effect of these positive feedback processes? Purposeful action-taking at BP increased over time. In a top-down command-and-control organization, the mechanisms to create alignment and coordination through vertical processes of instruction and resource allocation counter the requirements for creating individual or subunit-level autonomy and empowerment. In contrast, BP's organizational architecture, based on the concepts of space and support, continuously reinforced both individual-level action-taking and organizational alignment and integration, based on the strength of purposeful action.

Collectively, the concepts of space, boundaries, support, and direction provide the broad architecture of a volitional company. BP has implemented these concepts in one way; other companies can implement them differently. Nothing in these concepts is impractical. Any company, for example, can create a mechanism such as Peer Assist. Yet few do. If managers want to unleash the power of volitional action-taking in their companies, they must gather the courage for initiating the kind of transformational changes that John Browne, Rodney Chase, and their colleagues at the top of BP have done.

But overcoming the challenges of facilitating a bias for action in an organization is only one part of the purposeful leader's task. The other part is to embed the values of purposeful management into the organizational culture itself—and thereby develop the kind of volitional managers who make such an organization effective. People who feel intellectually or emotionally dependent, who like to be told what to do and prefer to operate in the safe territory of maintaining the status quo—they will not likely work well within the kind of organizational context we have described. A volitional company needs people who are capable of setting their own goals and priorities, and who have the courage to commit to those objectives.

Let us turn now to the topic of how organizations can develop such managers by making a bias for action an inherent part of the company's underlying culture.

Weaving Purposeful Management into the Organizational Culture

"Top management talks about middle managers taking initiative," one financial services manager told us. "They say that they expect us to be innovative and creative. But what they actually do and how they deal with ideas that middle managers present tells a different story. What is more, they are totally unaware that they neither take strategic initiative themselves nor want us to take any such initiative."

In most companies, leaders' rhetoric emphasizes empowerment of their people and celebrates autonomous action of managers. But the reality is often exactly the opposite. Organizational structures and management processes can support or hinder autonomous behaviors of managers but, by themselves, cannot sustain such behaviors over long periods. If a company creates an organization designed to empower people, it will likely see a spurt of initiatives as people exercise their newfound freedom. But that spurt will be unsustainable unless the company's underlying culture and values align to decentralized, volitional action-taking.

To unleash people's willpower, leaders not only must build an organization that supports the exercise of freedom and choice, but they also must embed volitional behavior as a central element of the company's cultural core. Ultimately, a company's culture (the shared values, informal norms, habits, and traditions surrounding the way it does business), not its structure (the company's explicit, tangible, formal regulations, rules, and strategy), stimulate and sustain a manager's courage to exercise choice and ability to enjoy freedom.

There are no quick fixes or hard-and-fast rules for creating such a culture. One cannot embed values in an organization through a short-term project or program. In companies like Sony or 3M, the consistent action of many generations of top-level leaders has deeply woven purposeful management into the organizational fabric. At GE Jack Welch spent two decades relentlessly breaking up corporate bureaucracy and insisting on decentralized initiative to release the entrepreneurial spirit of his managers. While John Browne has quickly built the organizational structure for supporting frontline initiative at BP, he has only just begun the long, hard journey of stabilizing the values to sustain volitional action of managers as a daily, natural habit.

Creating the organizational infrastructure by providing freedom to act, supporting networks and inspiring leadership is one decisive step towards a volitional culture. Yet, all these interventions work only if the company has already a tradition or culture of active management. If the company has not, structural management interventions lead only to superficial effects implying that managers start taking action shortly after they received new degrees of freedom. Later, however, there is a danger that their consciousness and awareness of choice starts decreasing again, they become insecure how to use their choices and fall back into their former behavioral patterns; unless the company develops a culture of choice and develops its managers. Unleashing the willpower of their organization needs a volitional culture and managers with the awareness, courage, and joy to discover and use choices.

Senior management will inevitably seek to and to some extent must try to restrict certain kinds of choices. It will usually do so both formally and informally by policies and procedures and by the culture it seeks to create to guide managers' behavior. Senior management needs to know what kind of culture and what kind of managers it really wants. It is easy to fool oneself, to believe that one wants managers who take action but to provide no guidance and support contributing to developing those managers' willpower and a culture of purposeful action.

We found considerable differences between companies in how managers perceive the support of their executive management. An HR manager of a small private bank in Liechtenstein commented on his senior management: "In our firm top management talks about initiative of middle managers. They say that they expect us to be innovative and creative and all this stuff. But looking at what they do themselves and how they deal with ideas from the middle, tells a different story. Last month the whole board spent days on deciding who will get a flat screen. This is just one example that says everything. I am sure that they are not even aware that they do neither take strategic action themselves nor or even less want us to take action."

A manager of a large U.S.-based food production company commented the lived values of his firm as follows: "Do not criticize. That is the message that we get from our executives. They are so caught up in defining strategies and convincing themselves that they are doing fine, that they just do not listen. They would be really upset if someone would start questioning or suggesting alternative issues. All information is filtered several times. There is no misunderstanding; they really do not want us to think and make decisions on our own. That is not the culture here. And it is they who shape the culture. At least we know what they expect from us."

Top management has a strong influence on the degree to which managers perceive and exercise choices, as well as their perceptions of demands and constraints. The culture and the degree to which managers form volition and take purposeful action is strongly affected by the philosophy of senior management. Although top executives decisively shape the expectations and habits of managers, we have seen only few who consciously take responsibility for creating a volitional culture and developing purposeful action takers.

Hilti's Volition Development Program

The most systematic and long-ranging management development initiative supporting a volitional culture and managers' willpower that we have found was launched in 1984 by Michael Hilti, CEO of the Liechtenstein-based Hilti Group till 1994 and since then the Chairman of the company's Supervisory Board. Practiced for the last eighteen years and implemented at a total cost of $16 million, this initiative fundamentally changed the culture and the behavior of the managers of the company and directly contributed to the explosion of new products that have made Hilti the world leader in its industry. "I want our managers to take responsibility for what they do. One of the central conditions for this is that they love what they do. The second is that they are aware that they have choices. The third is that they commit without reservations," Hilti told us. Even so, leaders can keep some general principles in mind when crafting a corporate culture that supports a bias for action. For example, they can:

- Integrate the values of purposeful action-taking—and the behaviors associated with them—into all the company's tools and systems.

- Weed out managers whose behaviors do not conform to those values, regardless of those managers' business performance.

- Consistently invest time, money, and effort into embedding and upholding those values—especially by reflecting them in leaders' own behaviors.

Hilti Group, a Liechtenstein-based manufacturer employing more than fourteen thousand people in one hundred twenty countries, has used these principles to instill willpower as a sustainable, core cultural trait.

Building a Culture of Willpower at Hilti

Founded in 1941, the $2 billion Hilti Group has for decades been considered the world leader in developing, manufacturing, and marketing premium-quality power tools for the construction and building-maintenance industry. Moreover, the company has always fostered a culture that encourages managers' personal choice and volition. Well before the word *empowerment* entered the management lexicon, founder Martin Hilti firmly believed in giving employees freedom and choice. One of his leadership principles, consistently emphasized in all his interactions with employees, was this: "You are free people. You chose to work with us. If somebody does not want to work here anymore because he cannot identify with his work or the conditions, he should leave the company. . . . I consider it my prime task to create a climate where everybody can and should develop a will and commitment to perform as well as he can, and to experience joy at work."[8] Even so, at the beginning of the 1980s, the company began to lose its competitive edge—and it was in danger of losing the volitional power of its work force as well. Rapid growth and internationalization in the preceding decade had made it increasingly difficult to sustain the creative energy that Hilti needed to develop innovative products. Moreover, the European and U.S. construction markets faced acute recession, leading to a significant decrease in Hilti's sales revenues in 1982—for the first time in its history—and the company spiraled into stagnation.

Hilti's top management was convinced that the company's business model—based on leadership in innovation, quality, and service—was unsustainable without committed and autonomous action-taking by its people. Management knew too that Hilti needed to make a transition from an era of distributed initiative, driven by the charisma of a founder-leader, to an era in which the fostering of people's willpower was deeply woven into the organizational culture itself. In a relatively small and less internationalized company, the beliefs and actions of individuals could sustain willpower and personal responsibility; in the large, global company that Hilti had become, that willpower and responsibility had to be embedded in the culture.

The management team began by introducing, in 1984, the core element of the culture-change process—the INNO training program—which to this day remains an integral part of the Hilti Group. With a goal of helping all Hilti managers strengthen their commitment, willpower, and action-taking abilities in their everyday jobs, INNO comprises three parts over a nine-month period. The program is taught throughout the company units in the same way worldwide and is staffed by specially selected Hilti employees. (The fact that each of Hilti's board members regularly conducts two INNO trainings per year attests to the priority the company places on culture.)

A three-day intensive seminar on the company's five core values—with five corresponding modules—kicks off the program. Workshops, films, and group discussions systematically make participants reconsider their jobs and everyday behaviors, to look at themselves in the mirror, and to rethink how they deal with responsibility, choice, and their environment.

Value #1: Consider Rules As Space for Action   Discussion of this first core company value centers around the need for rules to provide purpose and context for managers' creativity and initiative—especially when it comes to productive collaboration. But rules should not be viewed as restrictions; rather, they should focus people's attention on the opportunities and margins of play that the rules articulate. The challenge for managers, then, becomes learning to use the freedom they have to its fullest extent.[9] A second challenge is to consider rules in terms of a common commitment and to ensure that people can identify with them. In other words, Hilti encourages managers to question rules as well as to collaborate with others to shape and refine them.

Value #2: Overcome the Traps of Your Habits and Routines
In the second seminar module, managers discuss how old habits can hinder new experiences. The goal is to show participants that as managers, they can easily become a slave to their habits once they cease trying out new ideas and striking out on new paths. Such behavior can often create a vicious circle in which many managers find themselves making excuses for not taking initiative. In-depth discussions help managers conclude for themselves that, rather than their superiors or the organization as a whole, they are solely responsible for the positive and negative outcomes of their own actions. As one manager learned after this training module:

"It was pretty shocking to see that—in fact—I worked like a robot. . . . I had always wanted to lead one of our Quality Circles, but I never managed to give myself the necessary jump start to talk about what I wanted to do. [The session] allowed me to free myself of the habits that chained me down, and I dared to go for it. That was not the only thing. Today, whenever I find myself thinking, 'Sometime I would really love to . . . ,' I approach the matter with a great deal more awareness, and I think, 'Why do I not do it, then? What am I waiting for?' "

Value #3: Exercise Freedom of Choice: Change It, Leave It, or Love It   The program module focused on Hilti's third core value has proved to have the greatest impact on managers. In it participants recognize that they have the right to choose their own fate. With the catchphrase "change it, leave it, or love it," managers see that rather than slipping into passivity or waiting for someone else to improve circumstances, they alone should take action. One INNO trainer commented, "INNO's main effect is that we weed out all those constant whiners. There have been plenty of people who would say, 'Well, I would love to, but I just cannot, and the whole thing is only getting worse.' We clarify to these people during an INNO seminar that . . . they alone are responsible."

The awareness of the right to choose change has profoundly affected Hilti's culture. Two years after experiencing the INNO process, one participant told us, "My guideline for almost everything is 'change it, leave it, or love it'. Every day, I am confronted with situations in which I am not fully engaged in my work anymore and feel like tossing in the towel. But then I think that I must take things in hand and realize the goals I have set for myself. That mantra helps keep me going in difficult situations."

Value #4: Expect and Accept Setbacks   The fourth program module revolves around the core company value that taking initiatives and striking out new paths mean taking greater risks.[10] In this module, managers learn to change how they interpret setbacks and failures. Mistakes and bad experiences become learning opportunities that are at least as important as successes and good experiences. What matters is not making mistakes intentionally or out of carelessness. Those who give their all to realize something cannot make mistakes, in Hilti's opinion. Not everything always goes well, but that is not what Hilti considers a mistake. As former CEO and current advisory-board head Michael Hilti puts it: "The greatest mistake is to make no mistakes." In this module, managers learn that if they seek guaranteed success, they will almost surely stagnate in their efforts. Managers must deal with good and bad experiences with equal composure. Above all, they must adopt a new philosophy of regarding setbacks and failures as learning opportunities and use those opportunities as a source of energy for future action.

Changing an individual's perspective about mistakes is always difficult, particularly so at Hilti, whose premium-price strategy demands absolute excellence, technical precision, and perfection across its operations. Mostly trained as engineers, Hilti's managers have historically tended to see mistakes as personal failures. But gradually the program has encouraged managers to take more risks and to accept occasional setbacks.

Value #5: COTOYO—Commit to Yourself   The fifth module—and core company value—is a call to employees to fully commit to what they do. Through group discussions, managers learn how to accept and act on difficult challenges. The trouble is, the more demanding the challenge, the louder the little voice inside usually says, "This job is too tough," "You do not really want to do this, do you?", or "Someone else can do that."[11] During the training seminar, managers learn how to use their mental strength and willpower to squash that voice and take up the challenge of difficult or unpleasant tasks. This kind of commitment, made from an individual's free will, means promising oneself to take on the challenge—and to stand by it out of personal pride.

Embedding Values in Daily Behaviors

To what extent have these five values really become part of Hilti's day-to-day culture? In our conversations with Hilti managers in various levels and functions, two things were obvious. First, everyone we spoke to took the values very seriously. Second, they all believed that those values made the company unique and were the main source of its competitive success in an increasingly difficult global market. (For example, between 1998 and 2000, the company enjoyed a 19 percent cumulative sales growth and a 36 percent growth in profit.)

The following comment from a marketing manager was typical: "The culture at Hilti is unique. Its values are not what make it different from other corporate cultures, but the fact that those values are lived out. . . . At Hilti we work with a great deal of independence and personal responsibility. For example, we do not have set working hours. You go home once your work is done. The people at Hilti are not complacent . . . ; they try to solve problems instead of complaining."

As we mentioned earlier, several factors explain Hilti's success in using a training intervention to embed willpower as a core cultural trait. First, the company has integrated the values—and the behaviors associated with them—into all its management tools and systems. As a result, the values are always salient and are always in discussion. Second, the company has unfailingly weeded out managers whose behaviors do not conform to its values, regardless of their business performance. Third, Hilti's top leaders have consistently invested time, money, and effort to embed and uphold the company's values, in times good and bad. Let us examine each of these in turn.

Perhaps one critical management tool in which Hilti has integrated its values is the employee survey, which is taken very seriously at all levels of the company. Designed to monitor and improve Hilti's management system, the survey queries employees on topics from the company culture and working conditions to leadership and company strategy. Once analyzed, the results are distributed companywide. True to its value of "change it, leave it, or love it," Hilti places the responsibility for improving problematic areas on everyone's shoulders—from line workers to top management. Hilti's values are also closely tied to its systems for recruitment, selection, and evaluation of managers and for making strategic decisions and financial plans. By weaving those values into the company's regular management systems, Hilti's leaders have shown employees that the values are more than just words; they're something that everyone at all levels of the company must uphold.

Very powerful also has been the company's absolute insistence that managers who do not live by those values must leave the company—regardless of their business performance. As Michael Hilti puts it: "Our culture outlines clear rules of play. Hilti does not want managers who behave like stars or divas. Even top managers must act in the interests of the majority. . . . We are playing football. Those who do not want to stick to certain basic rules of the game and play tennis instead must leave."[12]

Weeding out such managers, however, has meant making some very tough decisions. As Egbert Appel, the board member responsible for human resources, finance, and IT, told us: "We have had to let go of people who performed well but who did not live according to our culture—people who tried to get ahead at the expense of others. The things these managers achieved were fantastic, but *how* they did so was not acceptable. Their behavior and leadership hindered others' ability to act independently. In the past, we never questioned managers as long as their results were OK. Today, we let go of people when their conduct violates our values."

Finally, another strong contributor to the creation of a volitional culture at Hilti has been the day-to-day behaviors of its top-level leaders. They have consistently embodied Hilti's values and have acted as culture carriers. This has not always been an easy task. A culture that emphasizes every employee's right to challenge management actions that are seen as violating a core value is also a culture in which top management must acknowledge mistakes from time to time. Leaders in such a culture must ensure that their own behaviors reflect those values.

For example, in 2002 top management's commitment to the organization's values was tested when the company faced the worst crisis in its history—a market downturn far more severe than the stagnation of 1982, which had triggered the INNO intervention. In 1982 the company had survived without having to downsize significantly. In 2002 it could not. For the first time in its sixty-year history, the Hilti Profit Assured Program—a set of cost-reduction measures that are automatically triggered in the event of a business downturn—proved insufficient for dealing with the revenue shortfall. Hilti had to reassign people to its operations elsewhere in Europe and in Latin America.

The executive board spent long hours questioning both Hilti's strategy and its volitional culture. In times of crisis, decentralized responsibility and employees' immense autonomy presented serious stumbling blocks. Could the company launch fundamental transformation measures and maintain its commitment to engaging the willpower of its people? Could the company take the high-speed action needed without switching to a command-and-control style?

The board unanimously decided not to compromise on culture. Appel told us: "To the contrary, we concluded that this is the first and most critical acid test for our culture. We will invest even more in it. We will respond to the challenge with our culture and through our culture. . . . We are going to all the decentralized business units and talking with people. They must understand the severity of the crisis and the reasons behind it to make the choices and build the commitment to solve the problem."

Ultimately, the performance of Hilti's managers demonstrates best the benefits of the company's culture of freedom, choice, and responsibility. Year after year, these managers—spread around the globe—unleash their willpower to set and achieve ambitious goals that keep Hilti's growth and revenues rising. CEO Pius Baschera described this power of engaging the human will as key to what has made the company continuously stretch itself, despite its market leadership and long history of success: "Many of our managers try to reach the stars and then accept that you cannot get there. Their logic? When you try to achieve 150, you will reach 140, while you will only reach 95 if you are going for 100. . . . Our people are driven by a permanent will and passion to improve. They are never content with what we have achieved."

Now that we have explored how volitional leaders cultivate organizational structures and underlying cultures that support purposeful action, we will turn to the final aspect of building a bias for action: unleashing the energy of the organization itself. How can leaders mobilize and focus the organization's collective capacity to act? How can they align and bundle the company's forces, creating a joint focus and fostering purposeful action throughout the organization? We will address these questions and more in our next chapter.

EIGHT

Unleashing Organizational Energy for Collective Action

At the end of 1991, Lufthansa CEO Jürgen Weber found himself with only two weeks of operating cash left in the till. After every major bank in Germany turned him down, he finally got a loan from a small East German governmental bank—and began the fight for the airline's survival. The process was stressful, and it tested everyone in the company. How Lufthansa's people perceived that period of difficulty interested us. As one manager told us: "The crisis pushed us to the edge of our capacities. It was hard, but nobody complained. To the contrary, we had fun. We achieved what we never thought possible. It is incredible what force was set free during this period." The result, of course, was that Lufthansa did more than just survive; it managed the turnaround and went on to become one of the world's leading aviation groups.

When Conoco, the U.S.-based oil corporation, decided to start a division dedicated to carbon-fiber production, management set the bar high: Not only would the division, called Cevolution, mass-produce this strange new material, made of lightweight and unbreakable fibers; it would do so at low cost. What Cevolution accomplished within just eighteen months after its creation in January 2000 astounded even Conoco's top leaders: The division grew from 5 to 250 people, a new production site was completed, and Conoco protected its new manufacturing process with thirty-eight patents. What was spurring such outstanding results? Said one Cevolution manager: "The possibilities are so fascinating and challenging—almost overwhelming. Everybody knows that if we make it, we are going to change the world. It is unbelievable what a drive this process has. The whole division is electrified."

ALTHOUGH THE TWO situations just mentioned differ—a fight for survival in one case and the achievement of a dream in the other—they share one important feature: They both exemplify highly productive organizational energy in action.[1]

In this chapter, we turn to the crucial final aspect of building a bias for action: marshaling organizational will to support the productive energy and focus not only of individual managers, but also of the company itself. We have seen such focused organizational energy in action—at Lufthansa, especially between 1991 and 1993 and since 2001; at BP between 1996 and 2000; at Sony between 2000 and 2002; in Conoco's carbon-fibers division between 2000 and 2002. Few can sustain such a collective force for long periods, and not every management team can inspire such force. Yet it happens, and companies achieve results beyond their wildest expectations. Looking back, those who participated in the process recall it as a very special time, even though they cannot always explain why. In each of these companies, *the leaders unleashed the energy inherent in their organizations*, thereby creating a strong collective force that fueled purposeful action-taking—and leading to extraordinary results.

How did these leaders do it? For one thing, they brought the organization together around specific strategic initiatives. We see this as a two-step process: first mobilizing the organization's energy, and then focusing it.[2] Later in this chapter, we will share several strategies for doing that, including what we call "slaying the dragon" and "winning the princess."

At the same time, these leaders appreciated that no company can exist in a state of permanent acceleration, continually striving for higher and higher levels of organizational energy. These leaders succeeded because they carefully nurtured their organization's energy in a way that their people could sustain it steadily over time.

Most managers have experienced the rhythms and cycles of energy in large organizations. They know that companies differ in the intensity, speed, and endurance with which they respond to threats, pursue new opportunities, and manage change. Many have seen the symptoms of low energy: apathy, inertia, tiredness, inflexibility, and cynicism.[3] These managers know that high-energy organizations can flounder if their energy turns corrosive: Their force goes into destructive actions and internal politics, anxiety and fear, or busyness and frenzy that add no value. By contrast, some leaders have felt the exhilaration of organizations that have fully energized around business goals and can pursue them with both vigor and joy. Managers know too that all employees have a reserve of discretionary energy, which—when set free—can lead to enormous effort and achievements.

Since assessing the organization's particular energy state is the first prerequisite for a leader to leverage that energy deliberately, let's look at the various kinds of energy that define organizations.

The Four Organizational Energy Zones

Have you ever worked in an organization where people seemed focused on the same overall mission and goals? Where the company generated innovations with exceptional spirit and perseverance—all at an astonishingly rapid pace? Chances are that you were working in what we characterize as an organization with high-energy intensity. These companies demonstrate high levels of emotional tension, collective excitement, and involvement in the company's goals. Their intensive emotional energy raises their level of alertness and urgency. They identify and respond to any weakness, process information quickly, and mobilize their resources rapidly.

You have probably also observed companies or certain phases in your organization where you felt that people were uninspired and not fully engaged in what they were doing, instead of being focused on a mission or goal. That kind of place, which operates at relatively low levels of emotion, attention, and activity, we characterize as an organization with weak energy intensity.

In trying to describe typical energy states of organizations, we have found it useful to frame them in terms of two characteristics: intensity and quality of energy. The quality of organizational energy distinguishes between positive energy (e.g., enthusiasm, joy, satisfaction) and negative energy (e.g., fear, frustration, sorrow). *Intensity* refers to the strength of organizational energy as seen in the level of activity, the amount of interaction, and the extent of alertness and emotional excitement. The intersection of intensity and quality determines an organization's energy state, which usually falls into one of four categories: the comfort zone, the resignation zone, the corrosion zone, and the productive zone see figure 8-1). The idea behind these four zones may sound familiar, from our analysis of individual managers' behavior—the frenzied, the detached, the procrastinators, and the purposeful action-takers. Though related, organizational energy is not identical to the sum of the energy of individuals. Long recognized by managers, the distinction between individual and organizational energy is now receiving more attention in academic literature.[4] Individual energy, especially leaders', influences organizational energy—while organizational energy affects individual energy.

While different departments in the same organization can sometimes function in completely different zones, most organizations function overall in one predominant energy zone at any given point. (The exception is a highly diverse and decentralized company, where the business unit may be the most appropriate

FIGURE 8-1

The Four Organizational Energy Zones

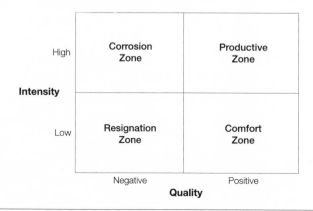

level for analyzing and managing energy. Keep in mind, too, that sometimes diversity of energy states suggests a need for greater intraorganizational integration.) The goal for any company, of course, is to find itself in the productive zone. Let us examine each of these energy zones in turn.

Comfort Zone

Old Mutual—South Africa's largest and most financially successful insurance company—operated in a state of low-level activity and emotional tension and high-level internal complacency for decades, until the middle of the 1990s. Populated with an almost entirely white staff, and with a reputation for being an upright and responsible company, Old Mutual was South Africa's version of the old Ma Bell (AT&T prior to deregulation of the U.S. telecom market)—dominant, comfortable, and happy with itself. Managers at Old Mutual were always polite in their conversations, avoided contentious issues, and worked at a steady pace without much stress or tension. Their pay, in relative terms, was modest, and they lived middle-class lifestyles. The company's financial results, while not spectacular, were about average in almost any comparison—and almost everyone, in and outside the organization, liked and respected it.

Corporations like Old Mutual that have succeeded for long periods within a relatively stable environment often settle into the comfort zone.[5] Characterized by weak but favored emotions such as calm and contentedness, they lack the internal vitality, alertness, and emotional tension necessary for initiating bold, new strategic thrusts or significant organizational change. Over time, these companies eventually become inert. Why? Because positive feedback and other signals of success lead them to perceive themselves as doing well, so they only incrementally strengthen their historically successful management systems. As long as the environment does not change too radically, this reinforcement and refinement work just fine. But, when the environment changes—as it always does—these companies find themselves as victims of the comfort trap, unable to muster the required energy for bold, radical change.[6]

Old Mutual faced this challenge as the South African economy began to change postapartheid. On the one hand, a rash of young and aggressive financial services companies attacked Old Mutual's dominant position in South Africa; on the other hand, opportunities opened up, particularly the chance to expand abroad. While the company has now developed the energy to respond to these threats and opportunities, its leadership had to act drastically—changing its legal structure, listing itself in the London Stock Exchange, establishing a new corporate headquarters in the United Kingdom, launching a massive transformation program—to force the organization from its comfort zone.

Resignation Zone

Companies in the resignation zone have the same low-energy intensity as those in the comfort zone, but the people who work there also find themselves in the grip of weak emotions, such as frustration and disappointment, instead of calm or contentedness. Typically, they suffer from low levels of emotional commitment, alertness, and effort. Since they feel maligned with the organization's goals, they often visibly distance themselves from each other and the organization in general.

Some companies fall into the resignation zone after change initiatives have repeatedly failed—leaving people feeling cynical and hopeless. Lack of transparency in change processes often has the same effect of producing collective disengagement and pessimism. Another route to the resignation zone is a long period of operating below capacity: The organization fails to exploit market potential and other opportunities, or it allows organizational problems to fester. Persistent mediocrity makes people in some companies lose their confidence in dealing with problems or challenges. Believing that nothing they can do would make any difference, they passively resign themselves to their fate.

SKF—the Swedish company that invented the ball-bearing business in the early 1900s and continued as a global industry leader throughout its history—has functioned in the resignation zone of weak emotions for almost two decades. Throughout this period, its performance has been mildly unsatisfactory—financially, it has been only modestly profitable, despite its outstanding technology, brand strength, and global footprint. Although its market share has declined, the rate has been fractional—managers could always round it up in presentations. Faced with low growth and languishing share price, the company has been incrementally restructuring for more than two decades.

An engineering company, SKF and its culture had always attracted technically qualified, mild-mannered people who disliked visible aggression or manifest competitiveness. Given the state of affairs, the company's managers had long been in a state of mild frustration and disappointment with which they had simply learned to live. Unlike companies in the comfort zone, whose inertia stems from the belief that they have found the ultimate success formula, companies in the resignation zone believe that they are simply not good enough to succeed. Threats or significant problems only confirm that self-concept and reinforce the negative spiral of hopelessness. Fortunately, SKF is now beginning to revitalize, and excitement is growing again. Sune Carlsson, CEO from September 1998 to April 2003, jolted the organization into more radical action—and since April 2003, CEO Tom Johnstone initiated an energetic change process involving an agenda for profitable growth.

Corrosion Zone

Companies in the corrosion zone show a high degree of energy, operating at intense levels of activity and emotional involvement. They draw that intensity from strong emotions, such as anger, fear, or hate. The interplay of high energy and destructive responses is one of the most debilitating energy states in which a company can find itself. With much of the company energy dedicated to internal conflicts, rumors, micropolitics, or other destructive activities, the effort needed to cope with fear, suspicion, and rivalry drains people's vitality and stamina, leaving little left over for productive work.

How does such a corrosive energy state emerge in an organization? Typically, the company faces some kind of external threat or opportunity that activates energy—but internal barriers, lack of integrity, or a general atmosphere of injustice soon deteriorate morale and team spirit. Most often, top management's behaviors lead to the corrosion trap, which reflects the inevitable mistrust and anger when patently self-interested actions of senior leaders, or their lack of personal involvement, prevent people from engaging in joint effort and commitment to a challenge.

That is precisely what happened to Westinghouse in the days of Paul Lego. The CEO's personal arrogance and isolation within a small coterie of favorites ultimately led to a complete breakdown of trust and alignment among Westinghouse managers. Each divisional head saw the others as his or her key competitors and focused any anger and dislike toward colleagues within the organization. Even though people at all levels of the company knew about the problem in Westinghouse's financing business—problems that would ultimately bring down the whole company—no one was willing to confront the CEO. By the time Michael Jordan took over the organization, the company was beyond saving: The corrosive forces of internal rivalry and distrust had gone too far.

With much of their energy dissipated through internal battles, finger-pointing, and stress, companies caught in the corrosion trap feel blocked from dealing with critical tasks. The accumulation of corrosive energy in a company follows a self-reinforcing dynamic that typically starts with small incidents. People unconsciously respond to others' emotional displays by imitating or exaggerating them. Unless forcefully stopped at the early stages, destructive behaviors of a few expand into a devastating force that spirals out of top management's control.[7]

We saw a typical example of this in 2002, at a large international corporation based in Europe. With the company clearly in crisis, top management successfully created a sense of urgency and a collective readiness to overcome it. People believed executives' vivid descriptions of the gravity of the situation and the need to stand together and fight; they, therefore, followed management's call for increased effort and were ready to make sacrifices. For instance, during wage negotiations, workers voluntarily accepted a moderate increase in salary of 3 percent. The situation changed abruptly when these same employees learned that board members had increased their own salary by 14 percent. The organizational energy quickly corroded, resulting in severe internal battles, calls for a worker pay raise of 17 percent, and the frostiest negotiations ever—accompanied by massive strikes. The crisis intensified until the top management team left the company six months later.

Productive Zone

Unlike companies in the corrosive, resignation, and comfort zones, those in the productive zone display high emotional tension, alertness, and activity. Employees communicate and work much more quickly, driven by enthusiasm, positive excitement, joy, and pride in their work rather than anger, fear, or internal rivalry. As we saw with Lufthansa, such intensive positive energy pushes these companies into exceptional productivity—operating at a high level of agility and using their strength constructively to pursue common goals. And as with Conoco's setting up its Cevolution division, typically these companies strive for somewhat larger-than-life achievements—extraordinary challenges that surpass the routine, the obvious, the normal. While low-energy companies look for standardization and institutionalization, avoiding surprises and risks whenever possible, companies in the productive zone thrive on surprises, the excitement of the unknown, and novel opportunities.

Take the example of Cartier, a French maker of luxury products, during the tenure of Alain Perrin. In the 1980s, this legendary CEO took the company from less than $50 million in revenues to more than $1 billion in less than a decade. As a young man, Perrin had arm-wrestled with French pop star Johnny Halliday, dined with the Beatles, and generally lived the Parisian life of revelry of the 1960s generation. He brought this *joie de vivre* to Cartier, then a relatively traditional French jeweler. Although the company competed intensely with Rolex, Chanel, and Christian Dior, Perrin never concentrated on competitors. He focused instead on creativity—on encouraging his people to design their own visions of the goals they hoped to achieve. Perrin's focus drew on a long tradition at Cartier. Jean Cocteau, the French poet, painter, and philosopher, had described Louis Cartier, the company founder and a jeweler to monarchs, as the "subtle magician who breaks the moon into pieces and captures it in threads of gold." Perrin focused the entire company on bringing that magic within the reach of all employees. "That is the secret of Cartier," he said, "We give everyone a chance to participate in creation."

Well-established norms within the company strengthened this creative spirit and the intensive positive energy it generated toward each success. For example, Perrin required that all new products bridge the tension between the old and the new. They had to capture the *zeitgeist* and form of one of Louis Cartier's early-twentieth-century creations, the drawings of which rested safely in the company's archives. At the same time, new products had to reflect some piece of late-twentieth-century contemporary art. Another norm dictated that new products must not reflect simply customer demand. "Cartier is a temple," Perrin declared, "and a product can be introduced only when it is worthy of the temple's seal."

Weak emotions are like moods. They do not spur people into positive action, where strong emotions might prompt impulsive negative behavior. Companies characterized by weak emotions, in other words, those in either the comfort zone or the resignation zone, operate at relatively low levels of attention, emotion, and activity. In contrast, companies like Cartier, characterized by intensive, positive energy display higher levels of emotional tension, collective excitement, and action-taking—all of which lead to exceptional productivity.[8]

One of the most striking features of companies during high-energy phases is their sense of urgency and alertness, which allows them to process information and mobilize resources rapidly. Inevitably, these organizations also have leaders who direct their people toward shared purposes, channeling the company's potential by aligning its collective perception, emotions, and activities to pursue business-critical activities.

Essential as positive energy is for driving corporate performance, unless one manages that energy with insight and wisdom, it can degenerate into severe pathologies. The greatest danger? Falling into the acceleration trap.[9] Seeing what companies can achieve in stretching phases of intensive energy, some CEOs assume that the exceptional can become the routine. Following the Olympic motto "always more, always faster, always higher," they drive their organizations constantly at and beyond the edge of their capabilities. This effort to achieve a state of permanent acceleration ultimately leads to organizational burnout.[10] The company and its people simply become exhausted.

Many companies fall victim to the acceleration trap because they mindlessly adopt one major change initiative after another, without finding time for organizational regeneration or recovery. Instead of assuming that the change process is an exceptional episode in a company's life, most organizations experience chains of change or ongoing change for long periods.[11] Under these circumstances, the call "to give it your all" is no longer credible, because people simply cannot give it their all, all the time.

ABB, the European engineering giant, suffered from just such pathology under the leadership of Percy Barnevik and a few subsequent CEOs. Barnevik's plan worked well enough in the beginning, when, between 1988 and 1995, the company responded magnificently to his radical restructuring. He reduced costs, integrated new acquisitions effectively, and rapidly built the company's position in a number of new markets. Over this period, ABB's revenue grew from $17.8 billion to $36.2 billion, while its operating income leaped from $854 million to $3.2 billion.

At the same time, however, Barnevik had put the entire organization under severe pressure—and the strains began to show. In the power-generation sector, for example, internal conflicts raged. The healthy tension in the ABB matrix began to degenerate into intense rivalries, and some of the company's highest-performing managers resigned.

A new CEO, Goran Lindahl, imposed his drastic reorganization on this already exhausted organization in September 1998. Once more, people had to change—forgoing the reporting relationships they had established with their geographical managers to report instead to the relatively younger, typically more ambitious and more aggressive business executives. At this point, the classic symptoms of organizational exhaustion began to emerge: poor prioritization, unrealistically high expectations, and scattered attention.[12] Under pressure to achieve radical improvements in a broad range of performance parameters, most of ABB's field managers fell into a state of frenzy, spinning their wheels aimlessly and achieving little effective change.

Sensing this organizational exhaustion, first Lindahl and then his successor, Jürgen Centerman, put even more pressure on the company. As performance continued to decline and ABB faced increasing media and shareholder criticism, the acceleration trap soon left the company little energy with which to revitalize itself. Fortunately, since September 2002, ABB has been undergoing an emergency change program that is rooted in a long-term vision by current CEO Jürgen Dormann—and is already starting to show positive effects: Within a year of Dormann's appointment, the organization's earnings before interest and taxes rose by 14 percent, and share price rose from around 1.5 francs ($1.10 U.S.) to 8 francs ($5.90 U.S.). Moreover, ABB has spearheaded several innovative projects, such as the world's longest underground power line (completed in September 2003), which won an engineering award. Most important, the energy in the company has changed—hope and some of the positive spirit have started to return—which has been widely credited to Dormann's positive leadership style.

How to Move Your Organization into the Productive Zone

Companies that we have seen achieve truly radical change had leaders who adopted one of three approaches for focusing the energy of their organizations and moving them into the productive zone. Some adopt what we call a slaying-the-dragon strategy, driving their people out of the comfort zone by focusing their emotion, attention, and action on a crisis or a threat to overcome. Others pursue a winning-the-princess strategy, mobilizing their organizations into the productive zone by building people's enthusiasm for realizing a specific, motivating dream. Others adopt a third strategy of combining the first two, and although we have seen this done less frequently, the results often prove stellar. Companies without either a dragon to kill or a princess to win inevitably fall into one of the energy traps: They gradually decline to mediocrity and eventually face a full-blown crisis.

Slaying the Dragon

Organizational energy is especially high and productive whenever people face a common, external threat or enemy. The slaying-the-dragon strategy relies on leaders focusing on two critical tasks (see figure 8-2).

First, you must clearly define and describe the "dragon" by identifying a distinct, unmistakable, and tangible threat. The threat can be bankruptcy, a particularly dangerous competitor, or a disruptive technology with the potential for making your company's products or services obsolete. To drive people out of their routines, they must not only see the threat but also experience it emotionally, in their gut.[13] The slaying-the-dragon strategy is particularly effective for jolting companies out of the comfort zone. The same strategy can misfire badly for companies in the resignation zone by driving them even deeper into the morass of hopelessness and frustration.

Second, you must direct the resulting energy toward collective action within the organization. Typically, acknowledgment of a threat creates emotions such as fear or anger. To convert any negative reactions into productive energy, you must show that joint effort can indeed kill the dragon. Fear and anger can generate optimism and enthusiasm only when people see the opportunity for overcoming the threat through integration, cohesion, and emotional alignment. Leaders who neglect the importance of channeling the energy generated by a threat toward a joint response typically find themselves in the corrosion trap, confronting the negative dynamics of dissipated or destructive energy.

FIGURE 8-2

Slaying-the-Dragon Strategy for Focusing Organizational Energy

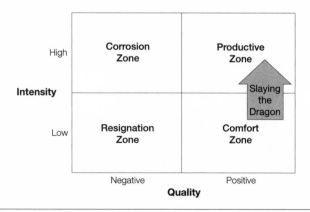

Take the case of Philips, a Dutch electronics giant. In July 1990 it shocked the financial world by announcing a loss of 2 billion guilders ($1.06 billion U.S.), driven primarily by the company's semiconductor division. At the heart of the radical turnaround that division would eventually achieve lies a classic example of the slaying-the-dragon strategy adopted by Heinz Hagmeister, the division's new CEO.

Jan Timmer, Philips's new corporate CEO, had already initiated one aspect of his strategy—activating strong, vivid emotions. In a meeting that later came to be called Centurion I, he shocked the entire senior leadership team by presenting them with a dummy newspaper report postdated by seven months with the headline "Philips declares bankruptcy." Participants in that meeting initially regarded the report in disbelief, but the actual financial figures Timmer presented soon revealed that bankruptcy was indeed unavoidable unless they cut costs immediately.

Hagmeister subjected his divisional management team to the same kind of shock therapy. Detailed benchmarking data vis-à-vis Motorola revealed dramatic gaps not only in inventory levels, sales expenses, and overall costs, but also in customer delivery and in new-product development time. Given the crisis in the overall company, divestment or even closure of the division was a real and imminent threat. Thus was the dragon defined in vivid terms—not just in managers' fear of losing their jobs, but in the shame and guilt of letting down their people and the company where most of them had spent their entire careers.

Having aroused these strong feelings, Hagmeister then channeled those emotions toward joint positive action to kill the dragon. He created a series of specific projects for reducing head count, cutting sales cost, improving delivery time, pruning the product portfolio, and integrating Signetics—the U.S. arm of the business—into the overall divisional structure. Each project had specific and identifiable ownership, milestones, measurements, and timing. A regular review process, called Centurion II, monitored the progress of each of those projects in minute detail.

Hagmeister himself demonstrated uncompromising discipline with rules such as "A budget is holy" and "Call shit, shit; call good, good." If an unpleasant task popped up, then he did it himself rather than delegate it. All numbers had to be exact: If a proposal indicated an inexact cost saving, like "between 2 and 3 million guilders," he would send it back. If a small location had a head count of twenty-six instead of the planned twenty-four, he would throw a fit. "There are no unimportant numbers and no approximations," he would say.

The result was spectacular. Within three years of the July 1990 announcement of unprecedented financial loss, the semiconductor division achieved a remarkable turnaround—from a loss of more than 600 million guilders ($320 million U.S.) to a profit of 340 million guilders ($181 million U.S.).

Because anger, fear, and hate are all very powerful emotions, the slaying-the-dragon strategy can be extremely effective in rapidly creating collective energy and channeling that energy into determined action. At the same time, however, this strategy has some inherent risks that limit its long-term effectiveness. One drawback of the slaying-the-dragon approach is that it can make companies myopic. With its energy focused on a specific, well-defined goal, an organization can lose peripheral vision. That is precisely what happened to Komatsu, the Japanese earthmoving-equipment company.

A whole generation of business school graduates is familiar with Komatsu's famous "Maru-C" slogan, a classic example of the slaying-the-dragon strategy. Faced with the challenge of Caterpillar's entry into Komatsu's protected home market, Ryoichi Kawai, the then CEO of Komatsu, focused the whole company on beating Caterpillar. "Maru-C" meant "Encircle Caterpillar," and, to make the "dragon" visible and omnipresent, Kawai purchased the largest Caterpillar bulldozer available and placed it on the roof of Komatsu headquarters. This story of how Kawai leveraged its aggression against Caterpillar into a highly disciplined and effective process of building up Komatsu's strengths and market positions has, for the past fifteen years, been the single most-used case study ever written at Harvard Business School.

What is far less known is the long-term affect this strategy had by constraining the ongoing development of Komatsu as an institution. Two decades of focusing on a life-and-death battle with Caterpillar prevented Komatsu from identifying new opportunities in related areas of business and from pursuing genuinely breakthrough innovations in its core earthmoving-equipment business. Finally, Tetsuya Katada, who took over the helm of the company in 1989, formally abolished the "Maru-C" slogan, and pulled down all the symbols Kawai had built to represent the Caterpillar battle. The result was the company's successful expansion into related areas, such as robotics, and a string of fundamentally different and highly innovative products, such as earthmoving equipment for undersea operations.

Another danger in slaying the dragon is that, when the perceived threat subsides, a kind of dead end can result. Believing that they have fought and won a hard battle, people and the organization want to rest and relax for a while. Too often, they then fall asleep! To some extent, Lufthansa suffered from this problem in the late 1990s. We described earlier the story of Lufthansa's turnaround from the brink of bankruptcy in the early 1990s. During the middle of the decade, however, the company's situation changed. Turning in record profits each year since 1997, the threat of bankruptcy no longer had any bite—and the company began to slip into the comfort trap. Then HR manager Thomas Sattelberger clearly expressed his concern: "Lufthansa seems to need a real or possible crisis or enemy to achieve quantum-leap changes." CEO Jürgen Weber voiced the same view: "Lufthansa has to continue in its success path and not become arrogant. The most difficult part is to keep people motivated now when the pressure has eased off."

To emerge from that trap, in April 2001 Lufthansa started D-Check—its fourth strategic change program since 1992. The program's purpose? To raise 1 billion euros ($1.2 billion U.S.) between June 1, 2001 and May 31, 2004—through cost cutting and other measures—and thereby prepare for all future risks perceived at the time. Little could the company have guessed, of course, how critical that change process would become: On September 11, 2001, just months after D-Check began, the U.S. World Trade Center was bombed, and the airline industry plummeted. Peter

Gerber, senior vice president and head of D-Check told us, "Before 9-11, not all employees understood that another change project was necessary. We were living in a lush phase and had slipped a bit into a state of inertia. The attacks caused a complete about-face. They transformed our world into a crisis situation from one second to the next. After that, there was no longer any debate about the necessity for change."[14]

Indeed, after September 11, Lufthansa initiated an additional change program, D-Check Acute, with a special focus on cash spending for 2002. Thanks to that program, which included security surcharges on tickets and cargo goods, the airline generated a cash flow of 530 million euros ($621 million U.S.) within three and a half months. Energized by external events, the program surpassed even its own goals: By August 2002 it had already met its objectives for all of fiscal 2002. By July 2003 the program had exceeded the total objective of generating 1 billion euros ($1.2 U.S.) until May 31, 2004—making Lufthansa one of the most robust airlines in the world.

Winning the Princess

Organizations can develop highly productive energy not only from the perception of threats but also from the belief in opportunities. The winning-the-princess strategy relies on leaders' creating energy from such belief in a vision for the future, for example, or in the potential of a new product, a new market, or a new acquisition (see figure 8-3). This strategy works particularly well for moving companies from the resignation zone into the productive zone. Note, however, that winning the princess is often less effective for reenergizing companies in the comfort zone, since such companies usually require a perceived threat (rather than a desired vision) to jolt them from their complacency.

The positive sense of urgency for winning the princess relies on strong emotions of excitement and enthusiasm to animate the company's energy. As with the slaying-the-dragon approach, winning the princess can work only if leaders portray the company's challenges in a visceral way. Making people see, believe in, and commit to a dream—something that, at least initially, exists only in the dreamer's mind—is inherently more difficult than making them see a real threat. Energizing a company through a desire for the princess is, therefore, a much more demanding leadership challenge than is using fear to goad people into action.

The key lies in defining, delineating, and communicating a specific opportunity that the company should seize.[15] You must create a clear object of desire—the princess to win—and make the passion for the princess strong enough to force people to overcome their resignation to the status quo. Getting people to attach themselves emotionally to such an intangible future means making the opportunity feel concrete for each individual; people must picture how they can personally contribute to the goal. You must formulate opportunities in convincing and personally meaningful ways, using a combination of simple, tangible images and a clear, basic message. You also must demonstrate your own commitment—by walking your talk and aligning your own actions and behaviors with the objective.

Take, for example, the way that Sony used this strategy to inspire employees toward a new vision. In the early twenty-first

FIGURE 8-3

Winning-the-Princess Strategy for Focusing Organizational Energy

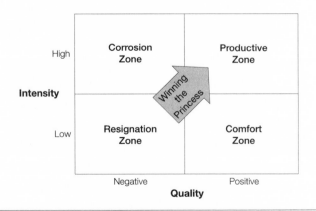

century few companies underwent as many fundamental changes as Sony did. Historically a producer of analogue-technology-based, stand-alone audio and video products, Sony was confronting a complete transformation of its business. The IT, media, and consumer-electronics industries were converging to a digitally driven, Internet-based, integrated-home-entertainment business. Accordingly, Sony CEO Nobuyuki Idei articulated his vision to enlist the organization in creating a new kind of personal computer: "Young and old alike are truly mesmerized by digital technology," he said. "These people, the 'digital dream kids,' are our future customers. We must also become dream kids at all levels of Sony to create something new, something that will meet our future customers' expectations." However, no one in the company responded to this first call to action from the CEO. Why? At that time, they did not believe the project could succeed; Sony had already failed twice in its effort to enter the PC business. Even so, Idei did not resort to issuing command-and-control orders. Rather, he became a source of inspiration. To make the "princess" tangible, Idei assigned Kunitake Ando (who later became Sony's chief operating officer), to create VAIO World, a virtual organization that allowed people to visualize how linking Sony's diverse offerings could exceed the public's future entertainment requirements.[16] VAIO World seduced people into the concept, so those who finally joined in did so as volunteers—because the vision captivated them, not because they got the task.[17] Although we cannot yet judge whether Sony will successfully manifest all of the visions that VAIO World stands for, it has already created the energy that yielded the new VAIO computer in 1997.

So, while slaying the dragon requires high-energy, brave, and commanding leadership, winning the princess needs gentle, inspiring, and empathic leaders who can unleash passion. It also needs leaders who create an environment of curiosity, excitement, and ownership, as Idei did with VAIO World.

Winning the princess is a long and exciting journey, not a fight, and requires exploration, freedom, and fun. In this strategy, people must perceive a margin of play for their own initiatives. Without this sense of personal freedom, no one can maintain the emotions of excitement and enthusiasm. For example, while a strong, hands-on leader himself, Cartier CEO Alain Perrin built his success on granting his people absolute freedom to craft new ideas: "A company is not only a money machine; it is a mosaic of men and women—a place where people live together, bound by human relationships within which everyone has the opportunity to express themselves."[18] Every year, Cartier's 4,600 employees generate an average of 1,200 new-product proposals in visible demonstration of their belief in this freedom.

Winning the princess requires endurance and the ability to cope with and triumph over difficulties. That is why, as a purposeful leader, you must also relentlessly build the company's belief in its ability to realize the shared dream—both by enhancing your people's competencies and by encouraging and supporting them. For example, leaders who talk about a vision for the future but spend all their time solving short-term operational problems do not build endurance or commitment to the vision. Perrin loudly reveals his commitment to creativity by spending more than 80 percent of his time on new-product creation—personally reviewing each of the 1,200 designs developed each year.

The Dragon at the Gates of the Princess

Each of the strategies for focusing organizational energy has its limitations, of course. Slaying the dragon relies on mobilizing often intolerable emotions and transforming them into productive energy for short-term problem solving—which risks neglecting long-term development. Winning the princess focuses on unleashing and leveraging energy in pursuit of a joint vision for the future but can detract needed attention from short-term problems such as efficiency and productivity.

Theoretically, an ideal strategy would combine the immediacy, decisiveness, and discipline of slaying the dragon with the lightheartedness, joy, and pride of winning the princess. In practice, however, leaders find it difficult to combine a top-down, planned strategy focused on survival needs with the experimentation, creativity, and playfulness of pursuing a long-term vision. Moreover, the contradictions and ambiguities inherent in such an approach can lead to the worst of all worlds, in which neither form of energy mobilization actually works. To some extent, Eastman Kodak suffered from this problem as it tried to battle Fuji headlong in its traditional photography business—while simultaneously pursuing the vision of building a leadership position in emerging digital technologies. In the absence of a direct linkage and positive feedback between those two strategies, the company suffered from confusion and a lack of cohesion for more than five years, leading to a stalemate instead of releasing new energy.

The only effective way to combine slaying the dragon with winning the princess is to create a path to the long-term vision that inevitably requires dealing with short-term threats and problems. That is precisely what Oracle CEO Larry Ellison is now attempting in remaking his company. His vision? To turn the IT industry into a utility, rather like electricity or water: The hardware, data, and applications reside in a central location so that customers can use them as needed—through the Internet. Oracle would evolve from a database company into a provider of integrated services, covering a full range of mutually compatible applications, including enterprise resource planning, customer relationship management, supply-chain management, and human resource management. Beyond its database products, customers can buy all their application requirements, all fully integrated, from one source: Oracle.

To Oracle employees, the princess is very clear. The idea of anyone anywhere in the world easily accessing the full power of IT with only a PC and a browser has enormous intellectual and emotional appeal. If Oracle's people succeed in realizing Ellison's vision, then the company will automatically emerge as the world's dominant software company.

Ellison has also built in a dragon. First, if Oracle achieves his vision, it will automatically impair its key competitors. With no need for complex systems integration, IBM will lose its main source of revenues. At the same time, Microsoft will cease to control IT access for business customers, and Oracle will replace it. Second, to convince customers of the viability of a whole set of standardized and integrated applications available over the Internet, Oracle had to become its own beta-test site. "Eat your own dog food" was Ellison's metaphor when he announced a target of saving $1 billion in costs—10 percent of revenues—by adopting this strategy within Oracle. The company did just that between 2000 and 2001, improving its operating margin from 14 to 35 percent.

Choosing Your Strategy

Not every company can be an Oracle, of course, with a free range of choice among the three strategies that we have outlined here. When a company faces a real and visible threat, leaders must frame it as a dragon because they cannot energize the company through powerful emotions when people are worrying about survival. Similarly, without an imminent threat, leaders cannot fabricate a credible dragon. Managers who try to create a pseudocrisis in such situations inevitably fail.

Still, in many companies managers can choose how they want to focus their organization's energy. So how do they decide which strategy to adopt? In our observations, external factors such as competition, market climate, and so on rarely provide a convincing basis for choosing one alternative or the other. Typically, the choice depends on internal organizational factors: the personal style of top management, the company's existing energy state, and the company's organizational heritage.

Perhaps the single most important basis for strategic choice is the style of top management. Based on their career experiences and personal preferences, most CEOs tend to lead one or the other strategy better, and they help themselves by being realistic and true to themselves. Slaying the dragon requires a command-and-control-style leader: brave, disciplined, and uncompromising.

Top-down instructions and meticulous plans fight threats. Winning the princess, on the other hand, calls for a leader who tends more toward an encouraging, empathic, and cheerful style. Command-and-control types cannot lead long and exciting journeys. A few chief executives can indeed create both princesses and dragons—Ellison is a good example—but most cannot. A company stands a relatively better chance of success when its strategy for mobilizing energy matches its leader's intrinsic style.

A second criterion for strategy choice is the existing energy state of the company. Slaying the dragon is easier to implement and more effective for unleashing energy in companies caught in the comfort zone. Such companies' state of relative satisfaction hinders creating excitement and sustainable energy by calling for a better future. Companies trapped in the resignation zone, on the other hand, already perceive a discrepancy between the real and the ideal. Winning the princess works best for them because it can more easily transform latent desire into productive energy.

Third, company history matters. Cartier's way of doing business had always favored playful journeys—creating magical new products that customers cannot resist. Winning the princess, then, comes much more naturally to this company that was shaped not only by the genius of Louis Cartier but also by the extraordinary group of friends who inspired him: Jaeger, the clockmaker; Lalique, the creator of luxury in glass; Edward VII, the then king of England; and Jean Cocteau, the painter and poet. By focusing on creativity rather than competition, Alain Perrin tapped into a company heritage forgotten in the postwar period.

———————

Both management theory and practice have, for nearly fifty years, adopted a very technical, analytical approach to success that has largely denied the role of energy. Yet, such "soft" factors as energy, emotions, and moods greatly affect companies' performance. Without high levels of energy, in particular, a company cannot grow, improve, or innovate. What keeps an organization from generating and focusing the energy needed to succeed? A lack of a shared purpose among its people—either a vision to attain, or a

BOX 8-1

Three Strategies for Moving into the Productive Zone

Slaying the Dragon: Unleashes organizational energy through a common, external threat.

- Clearly define and describe the "dragon" by identifying a distinct, unmistakable, and tangible threat.

- Direct the energy created by the threat toward collective action within the organization. This means converting emotions, such as fear or anger, into productive energy, such as optimism and enthusiasm that indeed one can slay the dragon.

Winning the Princess: Unleashes organizational energy through a belief in a vision for the future—the potential of a new product, a new market, or a new acquisition.

- Make people see, believe in, and commit to the dream by defining, delineating, and communicating a specific opportunity that the company should seize. Seduce, rather then force, people into getting involved in realizing the shared dream. To trigger their enthusiasm, people must picture how they can personally contribute to the goal.

- Help people overcome their resignation by strengthening their belief in the company's ability to achieve the vision.

The Dragon at the Gates of the Princess: Focuses organizational energy on both the long-term vision and a common external threat.

- Combine the immediacy, decisiveness, and discipline of slaying the dragon with the lightheartedness, joy, and pride of winning the princess.

- Create a path to the long-term vision that would inevitably require dealing with short-term threats and problems.

threat against which to fight. Purposeful leaders, therefore, must begin by understanding their organization's particular energy state. Then they must make deliberate use of strategies for marshaling the energy of their companies.

In this chapter we have shown how leaders can foster such collective action by focusing their organizations' energy, on either a dragon to slay or a princess to win—or both. In our next and final chapter, we will summarize the book's key findings—and show how you, as a manager, can unleash willpower in both yourself and your people by making simple changes in your daily leadership habits.

NINE

Freeing Your People to Act

A Mandate for Leaders

M OST CORPORATE LEADERS RECOGNIZE that people drive organizational action and, therefore, the performance of their companies. As we have said, for routine jobs—when the tasks are simple, short term, and involve relatively habitual activities—motivation usually leads to accomplishing them.[1] For most managerial jobs, however—when the tasks are complex and far reaching—mere motivation is not enough. Strategies that leaders use to motivate managers usually lead to superficial acquiescence to goals, rather than to conscious and deep commitment. Indeed, many leaders act as coconspirators with their people in developing a work ethic of superficiality. The result? Inauthentic consensus, smart talk, and poor action.

To create true commitment to an intention or goal, leaders must prevent people from superficial buy-ins. Building volitional commitment means making the process of signing on to a project more difficult—not easier.[2] Indeed, in our research, whenever we have found a frontline manager accomplishing a task with disciplined effort, we have typically also found a senior leader who had built in concrete steps to prevent superficial commitment.

We introduced our arguments in this book with the observation that such committed, purposeful action is a rarity in most companies. Then, throughout the past eight chapters we have seen why that is so, how individual managers can learn to act with volition—and how leaders can move their organizations toward such purposeful action-taking. Now, in this concluding chapter, we make one final address to top-level leaders of companies: What can you do to free your people to engage their willpower toward a bias for action?

Garnering willpower is a very personal, almost intimate process in which people tap into a very powerful force of human behavior. What follows are six strategies that leaders can use to help their people unleash that force and engage the power of volitional commitment.

Strategy #1: Help Managers Visualize Their Intention

Managers often have trouble committing themselves because they have only a vague idea of what they wish to accomplish. As a purposeful leader, you can help your people overcome superficial acquiescence by stimulating them to transform their ideas into concrete intentions. As Michael Hilti told us: "One of my guiding principles for leading people stems from the psychoanalyst Erich Fromm: 'If life does not offer a vision that one wants to realize, it does also not offer a motive to make an effort.'"

As we illustrated earlier, to build commitment, managers must have a clear and vivid picture of what they wish to achieve.[3] They must visualize not only their intention but also the process of enacting their intention. We saw how Jessica Spungin succeeded in creating this picture for herself to reach her goal of becoming a partner, but many managers—faced with a multitude of options and desires—need help simplifying their intention to make it tangible. As a leader, you can help your people develop the power of commitment by supporting them in the process of creating a vivid picture of their intention.

Consider Jim Taylor. Back in 2000, when he started building Cevolution, the carbon-fibers division of Conoco, he struggled with the fuzzy definition of his new product. Carbon fiber was a light, unbreakable, and noncorrosive material that had always been very expensive to produce. Taylor's division aimed to do what had never been done before: to produce these fibers in high quantity and at low cost. While he was convinced of the huge potential of this material (it could serve as a replacement for steel), he was having trouble getting started, overwhelmed by the sheer size and diversity of the opportunities. For example, the possibilities in transportation alone included reinforcing concrete roadways, replacing the steel in signposts, making cars with lightweight carbon-fiber composites, and so on. As he told us: "This material is so multifaceted that you can produce almost everything out of it. This was fantastic, but this was also the problem. I did not have an idea of what it really was. At first, I enjoyed this exciting feeling of the huge, undefined opportunity, but later I was not sure whether I would be able to 'get it down on the ground' and really tackle the problem."

The turning point for Taylor that finally spurred him to act came during a strategic business review meeting. Taylor explained in the meeting that, in principle, everything was possible—the product could become something really big. He then sought some direction from the senior team about where to start building the new business. Instead of suggesting where and how he should start, the group leaders challenged him to visualize the potential he was actually seeing. They pushed him to describe one concrete example of what this "really big everything" could look like.

"Slowly I realized that I wanted to build a bridge," Taylor told us. "I wanted a bridge to be made out of carbon fibers—light as plastic, hard as steel, a bridge that would neither break nor rust. That then became my personal hook." Taylor had a strong emotional link to his picture. His personal trigger was that he grew up in the northeastern United States, where he often crossed old bridges that showed the stress of exposure to salt air. Suddenly, he visualized how Conoco could exploit the noncorrosiveness by building bridges from carbon fibers.

After that meeting, Taylor began to build Cevolution with a persistent, sustained purposefulness—and to inspire that same kind of volitional action-taking in his people. To make the picture concrete, he told his division members to look at a map of the world and block off in their mind's eye every area lying within one square mile of any seacoast. Those areas, he told them, were where their customer base lay. The result? By mid 2002 Taylor had a process protected by thirty-eight patents and a production facility up and running. Moreover, the carbon-fiber business grew from a core team of 5 people to 250 people. Although after the merger with Phillips Petroleum Company in August 2002 management shut the division because of market uncertainties, ConocoPhillips continues to be recognized as a world leader in certain carbon technologies. Taylor does not regret a single minute of his involvement with Cevolution.

Strategy #2: Prepare Managers for Obstacles

To engage managers in a particular assignment, most leaders paint as rosy a picture as possible, downplaying potential obstacles and risks and highlighting the potential payoffs. They coax, cajole, and seduce their managers into taking on the necessary tasks. Yet, as we have pointed out, much of the superficiality in organizations arises from this definition of the leadership role as "persuader." Leaders who foster deep commitments in their managers see their job very differently. Instead of obscuring obstacles and downplaying risks, as a purposeful leader you must ensure that managers fully understand the potential costs and benefits of an engagement before they commit to it.

Sven Olafson, head of a European subsidiary of IBM, provides a good example of such a leader. Olafson had observed that many activities that were started with great enthusiasm at

IBM were often completed halfheartedly or abandoned halfway. Especially in the early 1990s, when the company was in trouble, multiple projects were started, but only about 15 percent were ever completed satisfactorily.

IBM had a Sounding Board that prioritized activities, decided about new projects, and allocated resources. Olafson noticed that project proposals brought to the Sounding Board were always overly optimistic and promising. Furthermore, they focused on business aspects only. To change all of that, Olafson introduced a new process for prioritizing projects. All proposals had to include information on four elements: business gains and risks, as well as personal advantages and disadvantages. Managers who presented project proposals had to answer such questions as "What would it cost me personally to undertake this project?", "What must I stop doing?", and "What else would I do if I did not take up this project?" The Sounding Board took on the role of devil's advocate—in terms of both business and personal issues. Candidates had to explain why they wanted to initiate the project despite the personal costs. When the Sounding Board agreed to a proposal, the process ended with a short interaction with the head of the board, who asked the proposer one final time whether she was sure she wanted to take on the project. The result of this new process? Far fewer projects were started—and of those that were, 95 percent were successfully completed.

Strategy #3: Encourage Managers to Confront Their Ambivalence

Volitional commitment requires that a person's thinking come together with his emotions so that the resulting intention exists beyond the reach of calculative rationality and constant cost-benefit analysis. But commitment cannot be found in the realm of irrationality or a lack of reflection, either. The difference between successfully creating a volitional commitment and not lies in asking the right questions. Considering motivation as their core task, many executives try to win managers through incentives or attractive rewards. Thereby, they encourage their managers to ask themselves, "What is expected from me?", "What is in it for me?", or "What is reasonable?" In luring them into doing something, executives systematically diminish their managers' ability to engage the emotional dimension in their work. Ultimately, they encourage superficial agreements and actually work *against* the formation of true, conscious commitment.

As a leader who recognizes the importance of preventing superficial commitment, you must force your managers to confront their ambivalence before deciding to engage in a project. That is a much more difficult way of winning people. But it is much more effective—and, in the end, less risky—than counting on halfhearted acceptance. True commitment requires that managers confront their emotions and reflect on whether they can personally stand with their head and heart behind an intention. To unleash such commitment, then, encourage your people to ask themselves, "Does this project feel right to me?" and "Do I really want it?"

We already recounted how Heinz Hagmeister transformed the fortunes of Philips's semiconductor business through his personal commitment and discipline, amid incredible odds. What was interesting as well, however, was how he became CEO of that business in the first place. When it became clear that the semiconductor business was in crisis, Wim Dekluver, chairman of the components division of Philips—of which the semiconductor business was then a part—decided that Hagmeister was the only person in his organization with the technical and leadership skills to save the business from imminent collapse. But for Hagmeister, the choice was far from obvious. A man of frail health, he was looking forward to early retirement. He had already built a nice house in Germany in which he planned to enjoy his retirement, and he had lined up a part-time job to keep him occupied. The last thing he wanted was to jeopardize his health and postpone his retirement by taking on the enormously stressful job of turning around what appeared to be a hopeless business.

Instead of ignoring Hagmeister's feelings, Wim Dekluver engaged him in an active discussion about the pros and cons of the difficult options. While Hagmeister wanted to retire, he also felt an enormous sense of moral responsibility for the business and for the people in it. He had worked all his life at Philips, building up the semiconductor activities: "I was a part of the management that caused the problem; how could I leave a sinking ship?"

That open and honest conversation with Dekluver allowed Hagmeister to ultimately recognize what he really wanted to do: to help clean up the mess to which he had contributed in the first place. By the time he decided to take on the role, then, he had confronted his doubts and resolved his ambivalence. That resolution gave him the strength to drive the change process that became such a success for Philips.

Strategy #4: Develop a Climate of Choice

The trouble with most managerial working environments is that managers have limited opportunities to exercise choice and, therefore, slim chances for developing their will. To create managers who act from their personal willpower, you must offer them choices, make them perceive and develop the courage to use those choices—and then step back. You must find new ways to support your managers' actions while not defining and determining what they do.

Earlier, we recounted the story of volitional action-taking of the Sony managers who created the VAIO computer. The VAIO was by no means an exception for Sony; the company's history is replete with stories of such determined and persistent action-taking. At the heart of this tradition of volitional action lies the company's rejection of a command-and-control model in favor of one in which all managers have a high degree of freedom in choosing their work and their careers. Sony engineers are not assigned projects by top management or by a centrally administered human resource organization. Instead, all jobs are openly advertised, and anyone can send in an application for any job. If an applicant is selected by the manager advertising the job, his or her current boss cannot prohibit the move. In other words, all employees have the right to be considered for the work they choose.

John Browne has created the same climate of choice in British Petroleum (BP). The company openly advertises all jobs other than the top two hundred in the 100,000 employee organization in its internal portal My Job Market. Any employee can apply for any of those jobs. Moreover, to broaden the pool of candidates, the portal automatically matches advertised jobs with employee CVs to alert both the individuals that might be a good fit and the advertisers about potential candidates who might not have applied.

A climate of choice involves responsibility and accountability as well as freedom to act. Involving managers in decision processes and providing them space also implies creating a climate of responsible action. That is exactly what Lufthansa did in its strategic change program, D-Check.[4] The need to generate 1 billion euros in additional cash flow within three years in a company that had already undergone a decade of fundamental change was challenging; success depended on all managers acting in responsibly innovative ways. Lufthansa's top management, therefore, created a climate of choice by involving the managers of all five business units and the corporate units in the process of setting targets for D-Check—and determining in real numbers the risks involved. The result? Managers felt that D-Check was not just a change program that upper management had invented and now imposed on them. Rather, they experienced the program as one that they had created to help ensure the company's future—and one whose outcome they were personally responsible for.

Strategy #5: Build a Self-Regulating System

The flip side of choice is discipline; if managers have the right to choose, they must also have the discipline to stop and rectify a wrong choice. Indeed, one fundamental problem with willpower

is that it can blind people, making disengagement extremely difficult and painful. Volitional commitments must at some time or
another end—whether because the intention proves to be undesirable, undoable, or simply done.

Yet, if that discipline is imposed from above—for example,
when a leader believes that a manager has taken a wrong turn—
then that manager will feel less inclined to exercise choice next
time. If you wish to create a true sense of choice among your people, you must also build in self-regulating systems to manage the
risks inherent in volitional action. For example, you can insist that
managers who initiate projects also take responsibility for deactivating them. Have your managers define—right from the start—
their own stopping rules: certain critical events or intermediate results that, should they occur, trigger the project's termination.

But what about highly innovative projects, for which defining
such concrete criteria for deactivation can be almost impossible? In
these cases, leaders can create certain "social stopping mechanisms,"
which have the same protective effect but are more flexible.

Lars Kolind, the CEO of Oticon, developed such social stopping mechanisms in this highly decentralized and entrepreneurial
hearing-aid company based in Denmark. The self-regulating company has no formal departments, and all employees, except the
handful of top-level leaders, are called "associates"—with no hierarchical separation. Any employee can initiate a project, as long
as she can convince her colleagues to voluntarily join the project
and get one of the top-level leaders to sponsor it. That is when
Oticon's social stopping mechanisms kick in, through one simple
rule: Any project will automatically terminate if the project initiator decides to give up, if the volunteering team members withdraw
their participation, or if the top-management sponsor backs out.
In this way, projects that once seemed promising—but later turn
out to be unrealistic or not worth continuing—are shut down
without leaving the project's initiator feeling that the decision was
arbitrary. On the contrary, the process is completely transparent,
minimizing political game playing and negative surprises, and,
therefore, results in less frustration for everyone involved.

Strategy #6: Create a Desire for the Sea

The French World War II pilot and philosopher Antoine de Saint-Exupéry wrote: "If you want to build a ship, don't drum up your men to go to the forest to gather wood, saw it, and nail the planks together. Instead, teach them the desire for the sea."

That metaphor reflects an enduring truth about building willpower: As a leader, you must create in your managers the capacity to dream. Many managers are prisoners of routines. They do not have time to dream. Some lack the openness of mind necessary for visualizing an exciting future and the opportunities that may lie there. Others may dream but kill those dreams immediately because they cannot imagine stepping outside their daily habits. Indeed, through their own efforts to systemize things, senior leaders often reinforce habituated work and prevent their people from taking the first necessary step toward building collective commitment and organizational energy: the ability to develop ideas and the capacity to dream.

There is no recipe for creating dreams; how can one find a formula for crafting a seductive picture in managers' hearts, a space for adventurous exploration? At the same time, leaders can follow some general guidelines for allowing dreams to emerge. The first requirement is to provide open space. As we have illustrated earlier, to be creative and, even more important, to engage willpower, managers must not only have the freedom to act but also *feel* that they have it. Leaders, therefore, must both provide managers that space and freedom in which to act, as well as convince their managers to *use* that freedom.

A second requirement is to provide managers with a challenge—a difficult and stretching task. Easy problems do not seduce or excite. They activate neither the intellectual nor the emotional levers of willpower creation. Difficult challenges do.

Finally, leaders must make goals or objectives personally meaningful to managers. That is why goals such as "maximizing shareholder value" can never lead to volitional action. To inspire managers, a "desire for the sea" can't be abstract or mundane; leaders must make the challenge meaningful and emotionally captivating.

Nobuyaki Idei made his company's challenge meaningful and captivating when he established his vision of Sony's future in the content-centric, Web-based new world of the early-twenty-first century. Rather than creating a strategy or a plan, he activated a companywide desire for the sea through VAIO World—a virtual organization that gave people from Sony's various product divisions a chance to be seduced by the concept.

The Foundation for Persistent Execution

Creative and breakthrough strategies, revolutionary change, the flexibility to turn on a dime—those are all very exciting ideas, and they easily capture the imagination of corporate leaders. Important as they are in their ability to occasionally catapult a company to very visible success, durable corporate progress is built on disciplined and relentless execution of specific projects and tasks. Unfortunately, organizational leaders themselves too infrequently exhibit those very behaviors—much less instill them in their people.

Persistent action-taking requires people to deeply and personally commit to specific initiatives and to undertake focused and energetic action to achieve their goals. That is the job of leaders: to stimulate the kind of managerial commitment that will keep organizations energized and continuously improving and changing. But all of this raises a broader question: Should leaders build their people's commitment to the company overall, or to specific projects or goals? We have found that broad loyalty to an organization is increasingly difficult to achieve and sustain. Besides, such general commitment, even if achieved, does not necessarily lead to purposeful action on specific tasks. A diffused

BOX 9-1

Inspiring a Bias for Action: Six Strategies for Leaders

1. *Help managers visualize their intention.* Encourage your people to transform their ideas into concrete intentions—a clear and vivid picture of what they want to achieve and how they will achieve it.

2. *Prepare managers for obstacles.* Instead of downplaying risks, ensure that managers fully understand the potential costs and benefits of a project before they commit to it. Have them ask themselves: "What would it cost me personally to undertake this project? What must I stop doing? What else would I do if I did not take up this project?" Then ask them to explain to you why they still want to initiate the project despite the personal costs.

3. *Encourage managers to confront their ambivalence.* True commitment requires that managers confront their emotions and reflect on whether they can personally stand with their head and heart behind an intention. Have your people ask themselves, "Does this project feel right to me? Do I really want it?"

4. *Develop a climate of choice.* Offer your managers choices and encourage them to use those choices—and then step

---

sense of organizational loyalty often creates a taken-for-granted kind of relationship between managers and the company that actually dulls the edge of execution.

The best way leaders can build effective organizational commitment, therefore, is from the bottom-up, on the foundation of back. Find new ways to support your managers' actions while not defining and determining what they do. At the same time, do not compromise about goals and performance standards. Make clear that choice is inevitably linked to responsibility—and keep people accountable by monitoring and supporting them.

5. *Build a self-regulating system.* If managers have the right to choose, they must also have the discipline to stop and rectify a wrong choice. To create self-regulating measures without arbitrarily imposing hierarchical authority, make any manager who initiates a project also responsible for deactivating it. Insist that managers define—right from the start—their own stopping rules: certain critical events or intermediate results which, should they occur, would trigger the project's termination. For highly innovative projects, where defining such concrete criteria for deactivation can be difficult, define a set of social stopping mechanisms that have the same protective effect but are more flexible.

6. *Create a desire for the sea.* Provide open space. To engage willpower, managers must not only have the freedom to act but also feel that they have it. You must also provide your people with a challenge—a difficult and stretching task. Finally, make goals or objectives personally meaningful to managers. A "desire for the sea," or way to inspire people, can be neither abstract nor mundane; find ways to make the challenge emotionally captivating.

---

personal ownership of and commitment to specific initiatives and goals. That is how Thomas Sattelberger became committed to Lufthansa, and how Matthias Mölleney committed himself to Swissair even when the company faced bankruptcy. It is how Dan Andersson has stayed 100 percent committed to Conoco, even after the company's merger with Phillips Petroleum Company—because of his personal passion to certain core projects, from breaking the monopoly in Finland to his most recent endeavor of establishing a market entry and expansion strategy in Europe. In the new world of mobile employees, corporate leaders must spur themselves to build such commitment as frontline entrepreneurship and constant organizational restructuring.[5]

In this book, we have explored the power of working with a bias for action on several different levels. First, we examined how individual managers can identify their own self-defeating behaviors and harness their willpower to become purposeful action-takers. Then we illustrated how purposeful leaders can shape the organizational structure and culture that will support such powerful action-taking by managers. Finally, in this chapter we issued a call to action for leaders to help unleash willpower—and, therefore, purposefulness and commitment—in their people, using the tools we outlined.

Ultimately, what distinguishes human beings from almost all other species are two things—imagination and willpower. These two wonderful capacities have allowed the enormous progress that human society has forged over time. Corporate leaders have many resources at their disposal—money, technology, manpower—but none is as valuable as their own ability to take purposeful action. Leaders must harness that same willpower in their people and instill a bias for action in their organizations. As we move into the future, this is *the* task of the purposeful leader.

How We Studied Willpower

O UR RESEARCH, conducted from 1993 to 2003, focused on two issues. The first dealt with action-taking by individual managers. The second dealt with action-taking at the organizational level: both how organizations could facilitate individuals' action-taking and how organizations could shape collective action. We studied those two issues in related but separate ways.

For our work on individual-level action-taking, we chose Lufthansa, a German aviation group, as our primary research site for several reasons. First, we knew the company well and had ongoing relationships with many people there. (We had written three case studies, one in 1996, another in 2000, and a third in 2003, describing the company's challenges and actions during the 1990s and early-twenty-first century. Moreover, many Lufthansa managers had participated in programs we taught at the London Business School and the University of St. Gallen.)

Second, the company has been the primary restructuring engine for the airline industry overall in the past decade by creating, for example, the Star Alliance, which changed the industry's competitive landscape from individual airlines to strategic networks.

Such innovations made Lufthansa a good place to observe what managers who display a bias for action can produce when no external threat calls for an immediate response.

Third, and most critical, the airline underwent a radical turn-around in the 1990s—from near bankruptcy in 1991 to record profits of 1 billion deutsche marks in 1997—which offered us an excellent opportunity in which to observe the extremes of management behavior. In 1991 Jürgen Weber, Lufthansa's charismatic and highly regarded new CEO, declared war on the airline's traditional bureaucratic culture, creating freedom for managers at the operating levels to take bold action. In fact, we found that Weber's ability to mobilize his managers' action potential was *the* reason for Lufthansa's successful transformation. Accordingly, Lufthansa —largely because of its innovation and change management competence—has most successfully coped with the airline industry crisis since the terrorist attacks on the World Trade Center on September 11, 2001.

In 1998 the Lufthansa School of Business initiated a program called Climb 99, which gave high-potential mid-level managers the opportunity to define and execute a project that they believed would help the company. We focused on forty-eight participants in the program over a two-year period, observing their actions, interviewing them in detail, and then using an elaborate computer-based program to analyze that information. One of the main lessons is that purposeful action-taking by individual managers is characterized through two factors: energy and focus. We then tested that framework by having those same managers complete a questionnaire that checked whether our interpretation of their behavior matched their own scoring on seven-point Likert scales. It did. Moreover, we found some powerful supporting evidence of what we had identified as key sources of energy and focus: ambitious goals, a sense of self-confidence about achieving those goals, positive work-related emotions, and the engagement of willpower. In this Lufthansa study, we also looked at what conditions foster a bias for action. We assessed the influence of different organizational factors on individual managers' action-taking. The results highlighted the important roles of space for autonomous action and the availability of social, emotional, and supervisory support.[1]

But all of this work was, so far, based on data from a single company. To test for generalizability, we replicated the questionnaire study at Conoco, the U.S. oil company. Here, we had a larger sample—250 managers—from a very different national, industrial, and organizational context. The results from this study fully matched those from Lufthansa.[2]

The last phase in our research involved responding to questions that resulted from our analysis and interpretation of the data. For example, how can an individual develop focus or marshal personal energy? We interviewed twenty managers—people we knew to have lost and regained energy, focus, or both—and wrote case studies on each, some of which we recount in part I. We developed that concept further through in-depth field research at several other companies around the world—all reputed as having created a context in which managers could take self-initiated action: Goldman Sachs, Sun Microsystems, and Oracle in North America; British Petroleum, Hilti Group, McKinsey, Micro Mobility Systems, namics, Siemens Nixdorf Informationssysteme (SNI), and Swissair in Europe; LG Group, Sony, and Infosys in Asia; and Natura and WEG in Latin America. The issue of willpower emerged from those studies as the clear and decisive driver of effective implementation of change initiatives.

In this phase of research, we focused less on the whats or the whys and more on the hows. How can companies create the belief that managers have personal control, support, and freedom—the factors that our empirical survey had shown to be the important organizational attributes for facilitating individual-level action-taking? What structures, processes, or mechanisms can senior leaders use to create that context in a company? How can they develop the kind of managers such companies need? We describe those findings on organizational architecture in part II.

When we originally framed our research, we did not include the topic of collective action; it emerged in the course of the study.

Clearly, something remarkable was at work in Lufthansa in the tumultuous period between 1992 and 1996, and again between 2001 and 2003. The managers who had lived through those periods told us about their strong feelings and unique experiences, but they could never pinpoint exactly what made those times truly unique. We eventually concluded that everyone seemed to draw upon and contribute to some kind of energy in the organization—not an individual energy but a collective energy. We saw a similar phenomenon at Sony, and when we compared that with Lufthansa and with our earlier experiences at companies such as Old Mutual in South Africa and SKF and ABB in Europe, it led us to the framework for unleashing and leveraging organizational energy described in part II. Our research into organizational energy is ongoing. We are now using empirical panel surveys in several global companies.

While our findings are largely inductive and derived from our observation of managers in many different companies, we have also drawn on and benefited from the work of many other scholars. We acknowledge this debt in our endnotes and bibliography, which we also hope academic readers can use to grasp the roots and linkages of our arguments in existing literature. Of all these debts, however, we wish to highlight one here in particular. At one time, the importance of volition (what we refer to in this book primarily as *willpower*) was widely acknowledged in the academic world. During the six decades since World War II, the topic fell into disuse as academic research increasingly focused on the themes of motivation. Only recently, a number of researchers in the field of psychology—Peter Gollwitzer, Heinz Heckhausen, Hugo Kehr, and Julius Kuhl, in particular—have reestablished the power and relevance of volition through their extensive and careful theoretical and empirical work. Their insights have been invaluable to us in interpreting and understanding our data, and we hope that this book will strengthen their call for greater academic and managerial attention to volition as the vital source of individual action and, therefore, of corporate performance.

NOTES

PREFACE

1. From C. D. N. Costa, trans., *Seneca: Dialogues and Letters* (New York: Penguin Classics, 1997).

CHAPTER 1

1. In many examples used throughout this book, names have been changed or otherwise disguised.

2. Laura McCormick's story has been adapted from "John Smither: Change Agent," case prepared by Susan Rosegrant under the supervision of Professor Todd Jick (Boston: Harvard Business School, 1990).

3. See Robert G. Eccles and Nitin Nohria, *Beyond the Hype* (Boston: Harvard Business School Press, 1992), 39.

4. Jeffrey Pfeffer and Robert I. Sutton, *The Knowing-Doing Gap* (Boston: Harvard Business School Press, 2000), 4.

5. See Thomas J. Peters and Robert H. Waterman, Jr., *In Search of Excellence* (New York: Harper & Row, 1982).

6. See John Kotter, *The General Managers* (New York: The Free Press, 1982).

7. See Dietrich Dörner, "Emotion, kognitive Prozesse und der Gebrauch von Wissen" (Emotion, Cognitive Processes and the Use of Knowledge), in *Enzyklopädie der Psychologie C/II/6* (Encyclopedia of Psychology), eds. F. Kix and H. Spada (Göttingen, Germany: Hogrefe, 1998), 301–333.

8. See Heinz Heckhausen and Peter M. Gollwitzer, "Thought Content and Cognitive Functioning in Motivational Versus Volitional States of Mind," *Motivation and Emotion* 11 (1987): 101–120.

9. See Jim Collins, *From Good to Great: Why Some Companies Make the Leap and Others Do Not* (New York: HarperCollins Publishers, 2001).

10. See Jack Welch, *Jack: Straight from the Gut,* with John A. Byrne (New York: Warner Books, 2001).

11. See Bernard M. Bass and Bruce J. Avolio, *Improving Organizational Leadership Through Transformational Leadership* (Thousand Oaks, CA: Sage, 1994).

12. For a distinction of problem-focused and emotion-focused support, see Richard S. Lazarus, "From Psychological Stress to Emotions: A History of Changing Outlooks," *Annual Review of Psychology* 44 (1993): 1–21.

CHAPTER 2

1. The origin of the word *emotion* can be traced back to the Latin word emovēre—meaning move, being moved. The terms *mood* and *emotion* are used interchangeably throughout much of the literature. See for example, C. D. Batson, L. L. Shaw, and K. C. Oleson, "Differentiating Affect, Mood, and Emotion: Toward Functionally Based Distinctions," in *Emotion,* ed. M. S. Clark (Newbury Park, CA: Sage, 1992), 294–326. However, we draw on concepts that advocate for differentiation of the concepts and argue that emotions are specific, intense, and related to a particular object (e.g., enthusiasm for something or fun in a certain situation), whereas moods are diffuse and unfocused (e.g., being happy). See J. M. George and A. P. Brief, "Motivational Agendas in the Workplace: The Effects of Feelings on Focus of Attention and Work Motivation," *Research on Organizational Behavior* 18 (1996): 75–109.

2. See "Sony: Regeneration (A and B)," cases prepared by Tomohiro Kida and Hidehiko Yamaguchi under the supervision of Sumantra Ghoshal (London: London Business School, 2002).

3. Weber (1922) distinguishes action from behavior in general, calling every form of human behavior "action" if and as far as it has a subjective "meaning" for the individual. The theoretical difference between action and general behavior becomes obvious when taking into account that Weber (1922) even considered "tolerating" or "desisting from doing something" as action if that behavior is subjectively meaningful. Max Weber, *Wirtschaft und Gesellschaft* (Economy and Society), (Tübingen, Germany: Mohr, 1922).

4. Ibid.

5. Basically, our findings are in line with suggestions of German action theory, which previously addressed the self-starting character of action. See Michael Frese et al., "Personal Initiative at Work: Differences Between East

and West Germany," *Academy of Management Journal* 39 (1996): 37–63. Crant and colleagues have emphasized the particular significance of energy as an element of proactive behavior. See J. Michael Crant, "The Proactive Personality Scale As a Predictor of Entrepreneurial Intentions," *Journal of Small Business Management* 34 (1996): 42–49; and Thomas Bateman and J. Michael Crant, "The Proactive Component of Organizational Behavior," *Journal of Organizational Behavior* 14 (1993): 103–118.

6. Although purposeful action is an individual construct where the consistency of personal goals is of main interest, we refer to *action* as a behavior within organizations that is also consistent with an organization's mission. That kind of action includes—from the company's point of view—constructive efforts to achieve a certain goal. For a similar understanding, see Elizabeth Wolfe Morrison and Corey C. Phelps, "Taking Charge at Work: Extrarole Efforts to Initiate Workplace Change," *Academy of Management Review* 42 (1999): 403–419. Obviously, managers can also take anticompany initiatives. That type of behavior is not considered here. See Michael Frese et al., "Personal Initiative."

7. See Robert Hockey, "Skilled Performance and Mental Workload," in *Psychology at Work*, ed. P. Warr (London: Penguin, 1996), 13–39; and Michael Frese, Marco van Gelderen, and Michael Ombach, "How to Plan As a Small Scale Business Owner: Psychological Process Characteristics of Action Strategies and Success," *Journal of Small Business Management* 38 (2000): 1–18.

8. Primarily in the case of low intrinsic motivation, a continuous strain of strong discipline and focus is most likely to lead to stress, alienation, and burnout. See Hugo M. Kehr. "Integrating Motives, Goals, and Abilities: The Compensatory Model of Work Motivation and Volition," *Academy of Management Review* (forthcoming); Julius Kuhl and T. Eisenbeiser, "Mediating Versus Meditating Cognitions in Human Motivation: Action Control, Inertial Motivation, and the Alienation Effect," in *Motivation, Thoughts, and Action*, eds. J. Kuhl and J. W. Atkinson (New York: Praeger, 1986), 288–306; and Lennart Hallsten, "Burning Out: A Framework," in *Professional Burnout: Recent Developments in Theory and Research*, eds. W. B. Schaufeli, C. Maslach, and T. Marek (London: Taylor & Francis, 1993), 95–113.

9. Bass has pointed out that, particularly in the case of precarious situations, managers tend to engage in poorly reflected, activity-obsessed behaviors that are coupled with a lack of goal orientation, a reduced use of information, and a superficial or diminished planning of activities. See Bernard M. Bass, *Bass and Stogdill's Handbook of Leadership: Theory, Research and Managerial Applications*, 3d ed. (New York: The Free Press, 1990).

10. *Procrastination* describes the phenomenon that a person knows what he wants to do, in a certain sense can do it, is trying to do it—and yet doesn't do it. See Bruce W. Tuckman, "The Development and Concurrent Validity of the Procrastination Scale," *Educational and Psychological Measurement* 51 (1991): 473–480.

11. Joseph R. Ferrari and Robert A. Emmons have described these two fundamentally different types of procrastinators. See "Methods of Procrastination and Their Relation to Self Control and Self Reinforcement," *Journal of Social Behavior and Personality* 10 (1995): 135–141.

12. Seligman introduced the phenomenon of *learned helplessness*, which refers to a manager's subjective lack of control. See Martin Seligman, *Learned Helplessness* (San Francisco: Freeman, 1975). Managers who suffer from learned helplessness were punished or suffered negative consequences at some point in their lives when they took initiative. Now they believe that any effort they make will be shot down. As a consequence, these managers perceive obstacles as insuperable, and they concentrate their attention and energy more and more on potential problems. They think they have no control or power over events, so they do nothing, which can ultimately debilitate their companies.

13. Defensive avoidance involves a *functional blindness*—i.e., a denial of the need for changes. See Donald B. Bibeault, *Corporate Turnaround: How Managers Turn Losers into Winners* (New York: McGraw-Hill, 1982). It can appear in different behavioral forms, such as living in the future, blocking or destroying information that conflicts with the present paradigm, sticking to the old paradigm, or calling for a "back to the basics." See Danny Miller and Peter H. Friesen, "Archetypes of Organizational Transition," *Administrative Science Quarterly* 25 (1980): 263–299. Janis and Mann identify those behavioral tendencies as symptoms of psychological mechanisms that provide a psychological defense as an alternative to coping actively with the perceived threat. See Irving L. Janis and Leon Mann, *Decision Making: A Psychological Analysis of Conflict, Choice, and Commitment* (New York: The Free Press, 1977).

14. See Michael Frese and Dieter Zapf, "Action As the Core of Work Psychology: A German Approach," in *Handbook of Industrial and Organizational Psychology* 2d ed., eds. H. C. Triandis, M. D. Dunnette, and L. M. Hough (Palo Alto, CA: Consulting Psychologists Press, 1994), 271–340.

15. Several theorists emphasize that crises in particular cause the desire for prompt, decisive, and often poorly reflected activity. See, for example, John P. Kotter, "Leading Change: Why Transformation Efforts Fail," *Harvard Business Review* (March–April 1995): 59–67.

16. German action psychology introduced the term *use of templates*, in which a person applies behavioral templates instead of generating new action plans through thinking. See Dietrich Dörner and Thea Stäudel, "Emotion und Kognition (Emotion and Cognition)," in *Enzyklopädie der Psychologie C/IV/3* (Encyclopedia of Psychology), ed. K. Scherer (Göttingen, Germany: Hogrefe, 1990), 293–343.

17. *Thematic straying* describes a behavioral phenomenon implying superficial acting and diverted attention. It is likely to occur when someone pursues many different objectives with roughly the same priority. Individuals who exhibit thematic straying tend to have intense inner conversations on the advantages and disadvantages of different alternatives. See Dietrich Dörner at al., "Ein System zur Handlungsregulation oder: Die Interaktion von Emotion, Kognition und Motivation (A System for Regulating Action or: The Interaction of Emotions, Cognitions and Motivation)," in *Denken und Fühlen: Aspekte kognitiv-emotionaler Wechselwirkung* (Thinking and Feeling: Aspects of Cognitive-Emotional Interaction), ed. E. Roth (Berlin: Springer, 1989).

18. See "Lufthansa 2000: Maintaining the Change Momentum," case study prepared by Heike Bruch and Sumantra Ghoshal (London: London Business School, 2000).

19. See Michael Frese et al., "Personal Initiative."

20. Our research focuses on factors that belong to the so-called action hub—i.e., more-specific personal states (cognitive, emotional, and volitional factors), which directly influence managerial behavior. These variables explain a larger share of the variance in managerial behavior than more-general personality traits, the influence of which on action is moderated through a number of intervening variables. See Edward A. Locke, "The Motivation Sequence, the Motivation Hub, and the Motivation Core," *Organizational Behavior and Human Decision Processes* 50 (1991): 288–299.

CHAPTER 3

1. Cognitive factors such as ambitious goals and self-efficacy energize a person and are likely to influence his or her will to enact a certain intention. See Edward A. Locke et al., "Effect of Self-Efficacy, Goal, and Task Strategies on Task Performance," *Organizational Behavior and Human Performance* 19 (1984): 135–158.

2. Social psychologists have long argued that individuals' affective state and emotional dispositions are crucial for the enactment of intentions. See Walter N. Mischel, Nancy Cantor, and Shel Feldman, "Principles of Self-Regulation: The Nature of Willpower and Self-Control," in *Social Psychology:*

Handbook of Basic Principles, ed. A. Kruglanski (New York: The Guilford Press, 1996), 329–360. A number of studies show that negative task-related emotions undermine the enactment of an intention. For a review, see Quy Nguyen Huy, "Emotional Balancing of Organizational Continuity and Radical Change: The Contribution of Middle Managers," *Administrative Science Quarterly* 47 (2002): 31–69. Conversely, there is also considerable empirical evidence to show that positive task-related emotions have strong, positive influence on action-taking. See Alice M. Isen and Robert A. Baron, "Positive Affect As a Factor in Organizational Behavior," *Research in Organizational Behavior* 13 (1991): 1–53. For a review of the relevant literature, see Heike Bruch, *Leaders' Action: Model Development and Testing* (Munich: Hampp, 2003).

3. See Edwin A. Locke and Gary P. Latham, *A Theory of Goal Setting and Task Performance* (Englewood Cliffs, NJ: Prentice-Hall, 1990).

4. See Albert Bandura, *Self-Efficacy: The Expertise of Control* (New York: Freeman, 1997).

5. See "Lufthansa 2003: Energising a Decade of Change," case prepared by Heike Bruch (St. Gallen, Switzerland: University of St. Gallen, 2003).

6. Research in the field of emotion psychology indicates that positive and negative affect are independent personal states. Watson, Clark, and Tellegen introduced a measure of positive and negative affect in which positive affect (PA) reflects the extent to which a person feels enthusiastic, active, and alert. High PA is a state of high energy, full concentration, and pleasurable engagement, whereas low PA is characterized by sadness and lethargy. In contrast, negative affect (NA) is a general dimension of subjective distress and unpleasurable engagement that subsumes a variety of aversive emotional states, including anger, contempt, disgust, guilt, fear, and nervousness, with low NA being a state of calmness and serenity. See David Watson, Lee Anna Clark, and Auke Tellegen, "Development and Validation of Brief Measures of Positive and Negative Affect: The PANAS Scales," *Journal of Personality and Social Psychology* 54 (1988): 1063–1070.

7. See "Managing Change in the Computer Industry: The Case of Siemens Nixdorf International," case study prepared by Daniele Filippone, Riccardo Gastando, and Dimitrios Protogirou under the supervision of Sumantra Ghoshal (London: London Business School, 1997).

8. For the importance of self-efficacy as a driver of initiative, see Michael Frese et al., "Personal Initiative at Work: Differences Between East and West Germany," *Academy of Management Journal* 39 (1996): 37–63.

9. German action theory suggests that insufficient control can lead to increased inner orientation and anxiety. When a lack of control occurs in combination with high complexity of tasks or pressure, it will likely induce stress. See Michael Frese and Dieter Zapf, "Action As the Core of Work Psychology: A German Approach," in *Handbook of Industrial and Organizational Psychology*, 2d ed., eds. H. C. Triandis, M. D. Dunnette, and L. M. Hough (Palo Alto, CA: Consulting Psychologists Press, 1994), 271–340. Stress theory underlines this observation, arguing that distress is often coupled with negative emotional effects such as exhaustion, fear, depression, or dissatisfaction. See Richard S. Lazarus, "From Psychological Stress to Emotions: A History of Changing Outlooks," *Annual Review of Psychology* 44 (1993): 1–21.

10. Social support—especially ties that are high in trust—help buffer negative experiences, allowing a person to cope with stress and reduce negative emotions. See James S. House, Debra Umberson, and Karl Landis, "Structures and Processes of Social Support," *Annual Review of Psychology* 14 (1988): 293–318. Emotion-focused coping is supported by informative and emotional support, which directly facilitates a person's ability to deal with his emotions. See Richard S. Lazarus and Susan Folkman, *Stress, Appraisal and Coping* (New York: Springer, 1984).

11. For volitional shielding strategies in general and emotion control that supports the reduction of negative emotions, see Julius Kuhl, *Motivation, Conflict, and Action Control* (Berlin: Springer, 1983).

12. For the characteristics of energizing goals, see Locke and Latham, *A Theory of Goal Setting and Task Performance*.

13. Our quantitative empirical studies on the emergence of managers' purposeful action repeatedly indicate that certain contextual factors (controllability, inspiring leadership, and both emotional and professional support) have a strong indirect influence on the emergence of action but do not influence the degree to which managers take purposeful action or their volition directly. Rather contextual factors have an indirect effect on action and willpower because they can induce the cognitive and emotional energy, which managers need for action and willpower—i.e., his or her self-efficacious aspiration and positive task-related emotions. See Heike Bruch and Sumantra Ghoshal, "Managerial Action: Construct Definition, Model Development and Testing," working paper, University of St. Gallen, St. Gallen, Switzerland 2003.

14. We later discuss Narziss Ach's theory of the will, which suggests that the more precise and substantiated the notions of an intention are, the stronger a person's tendency to carry out that intended action. A central

finding of Ach's experiments was the "principle of specific determination," which states that the speed and likelihood of enactment of an intention are positive functions of its specificity. See Narziss Ach, *Analyse des Willens* (Analysis of the Will) (Berlin: Urban & Schwarzenberg, 1935). A more recent discussion of the determinants of the intention-behavior relation confirmed his findings. See Icek Ajzen and Martin Fishbein, "Attitude-Behavior Relations: A Theoretical Analysis and Review of Empirical Research," *Psychological Bulletin* 84 (1977): 888–918.

15. Gollwitzer and colleagues suggested that a supplemental intention—called *implementation intention*—helps people recognize opportunities and get started on their action. See Veronika Brandstätter, Angelika Lengfelder, and Peter M. Gollwitzer, "Implementation Intentions and Efficient Action Initiation," *Journal of Personality and Social Psychology* 81 (2001): 946–960 and Peter M. Gollwitzer, Heinz Heckhausen, and Heike Ratajczak, "From Weighing to Willing: Approaching a Change Decision Through Pre- or Postdecisional Mentation," *Organizational Behavior and Human Decision Processes* 45 (1990): 41–65.

16. See Jürgen Beckmann and Miguel Kazén, "Action and State Orientation and the Performance of Top Athletes," in *Volition and Personality: Action Versus State Orientation*, eds. J. Kuhl and J. Beckmann (Seattle and Bern, Switzerland: Hogrefe & Huber, 1994), 439–451.

17. In the case of indoctrinated goals, the process of commitment building will likely cease. See Julius Kuhl and Thomas Goschke, "A Theory of Action Control: Mental Subsystems, Modes of Control, and Volitional Conflict Resolution Strategies," in *Volition and Personality*, 93–124.

18. See Heinz Heckhausen and Peter M. Gollwitzer, "Thought Content and Cognitive Functioning in Motivational Versus Volitional States of Mind," *Motivation and Emotion* 11 (1987): 101–120.

19. Regardless of how capable someone really is, that person will unlikely perform a task well if he does not believe that he is capable of doing so. See Jean M. Phillips and Stanley M. Gully, "Role of Goal Orientation, Ability, Need for Achievement, and Locus of Control in the Self-Efficacy and Goal-Setting Process," *Journal of Applied Psychology* 82 (1997): 792–802.

CHAPTER 4

1. The Rubicon model was introduced by Heinz Heckhausen and colleagues. For one of the foundational pieces of this stream of work, see H. Heckhausen and J. Kuhl, "From Wishes to Action: The Dead Ends and Short Cuts on the Long Way to Action," in *Goal Directed Behavior: The Concept of Action in Psychology*, eds. M. Frese and J. Sabini (Hillsdale, NJ:

Erlbaum, 1985), 134–159. For a more detailed discussion on the distinction between motivation and volition, see Heinz Heckhausen and Peter M. Gollwitzer, "Thought Content and Cognitive Functioning in Motivational Versus Volitional States of Mind," *Motivation and Emotion* 11 (1987): 101–120.

2. See Narziss Ach, *Über den Willensakt und das Temperament: Eine experimentelle Untersuchung* (On the Act of the Will and Temperament: An Experimental Study) (Leipzig, Germany: Quelle & Meyer, 1910).

3. See Kurt Lewin, "Field Theory in Social Science," in *Selected Theoretical Papers*, ed. D. Cartwright (New York: Harper, 1951).

4. See Arthur Schopenhauer, *Die Welt als Wille und Vorstellung* (The World as Will and Idea) (Cologne, Germany: Könemann, 1997). The last and third edition of the book was published in 1856 and Friedrich Nietzsche, *Der Wille zur Macht* (The Will to Power) (Stuttgart, Germany: Kröner, 1996). The title *The Will to Power* was the name that Nietzsche gave to a proposed book during his final period of work between 1883 and 1888. He never completed the book, but a collection of his fragments was put together by editors under that title.

5. Heckhausen analyzed the use of the terms *will* and *volition* in psychological abstracts. He found out that in the late nineteenth century and in the early twentieth century, *will* and *volition* were well-established key words of psychological literature. In the first volume of *Psychological Abstracts* from 1927, about four per thousand of the entries contained *will* or *volition*. In 1930 a rapid downturn started. In 1945 *volition* and in 1970 *will* were cancelled completely. See Heinz Heckhausen, "Perspektiven der Psychologie des Wollens (Perspectives of a Psychology of the Will)," in *Jenseits des Rubikon: Der Wille in der Humanwissenschaft* (Beyond the Rubicon: The Will in Human Sciences), eds. H. Heckhausen; P. M. Gollwitzer, and F. E. Weinert (Berlin and Heidelberg, Germany: Springer, 1987), 143–175.

6. The distinction between volition and motivation was largely lost after World War II, until recently when a group of German researchers returned to it. In fact, a school of volition research exists now in Germany. For a detailed discussion on the distinction between motivation and volition, see Heckhausen and Gollwitzer, "Thought Content and Cognitive Functioning."

7. See Edward L. Deci, *Why We Do What We Do: Understanding Self-Motivation* (New York: Putnam, 1995); and Kenneth W. Thomas, *Intrinsic Motivation at Work: Building Energy & Commitment* (San Francisco: Berrett-Koehler, 2000).

8. See Jim Collins, *From Good to Great: Why Some Companies Make the Leap and Others Do Not* (New York: HarperCollins Publishers, 2001).

9. See Peter M. Gollwitzer, Heinz Heckhausen, and Heike Ratajczak, "From Weighing to Willing: Approaching a Change Decision Through Pre- or Postdecisional Mentation," *Organizational Behavior and Human Decision Processes* 45 (1990): 41–65.

10. See "Micro Mobility Systems: Realizing the Scooter Dream," case study prepared by Heike Bruch, Beatrice Heim, Matthias Hofer, Daniel Keibach, and Michael Rist (St. Gallen, Switzerland: University of St. Gallen, 2002).

11. The debate on free will has emphasized the importance of choice for the emergence of volition and responsibility. See Harry Binswanger, "Volition and Cognitive Self-Regulation," *Organizational Behavior and Human Decision Processes* 50 (1991): 154–178.

12. The importance of free and informed choice as the basis of committed action was highlighted by Chris Argyris in *Reasoning, Learning and Action: Individual and Organizational* (San Francisco: Jossey-Bass, 1982).

13. Kuhl and colleagues developed the theory of action control, which implies different strategies for shielding an intention during the process of enactment: They termed these strategies *motivation control, emotion control, attention control, decision control,* and *context control.* See Julius Kuhl and Arno Fuhrmann, "Decomposing Self-Regulation and Self-Control: The Volitional Components Inventory," in *Motivation and Self-Regulation Across the Life Span*, eds. J. Heckhausen and C. S. Dweck (Cambridge, England: Cambridge University Press, 1998), 15–49; and Julius Kuhl, "Action Control: The Maintenance of Motivational States," in *Motivation, Intention, and Volition*, eds. F. Halish and J. Kuhl (Berlin and Heidelberg, Germany: Springer, 1987), 279–291.

14. See Albert Bandura, "Self-Efficacy Mechanisms in Human Agency," *American Psychologist* 37 (1982): 122–147.

15. See Howard Leventhal and Klaus R. Scherer, "The Relationship of Emotion to Cognition: A Functional Approach to a Semantic Controversy," *Cognition and Emotion* 1 (1987): 3–28; and S. E. Taylor and S. K. Schneider, "Coping and the Simulation of Events," *Social Cognition* 7 (1989): 174–194.

16. It has been suggested that volition contributes to overcoming deactivation deficits. Deactivation deficits involve both premature deactivation and difficulty in detaching oneself from a certain activity, including problems with starting a new one. See Jürgen Beckmann, "Volition Correlates of Action Versus State Orientation," in *Volition and Personality*, eds. J. Kuhl and J. Beckmann (Göttingen, Germany: Hogrefe, 1994): 155–166.

Difficulties in detaching oneself imply two phenomena: first, getting stuck in unfruitful behavioral sequences and being unable to "cut one's losses" in situations in which the aim has become unattainable and, second, perfectionism—i.e., a strong tendency to insist on intention realization although it has already been achieved. See Heinz Heckhausen, *Motivation and Action*, 2d ed. (Berlin: Springer, 1991).

CHAPTER 5

1. Psychologists speak of the "appraising character" of emotions. A distinctive feature of the appraising character is an intuitive and holistic access to understanding and evaluating problems. Emotions allow one to differentiate quickly between good and bad in terms of the relevance to personal goals, well-being, potential failures, and anticipated outcomes. See R. L. Atkinson, "Emotions," in *Hilgard's Introduction to Psychology*, 12th ed., eds. R. L. Atkinson et al. (Fort Worth, TX: Harcourt Brace College Publisher, 1996), 378–407.

2. For the effect of mental representations, see Peter M. Gollwitzer, "Goal Achievement: The Role of Intentions," *European Review of Social Psychology* 4 (1993): 141–185.

3. See Robert A. Emmons and Laura A. King, "Conflict Among Personal Strivings: Immediate and Long-Term Implications for Psychological and Physical Well-Being," *Journal of Personality and Social Psychology* 54 (1988): 1040–1048.

4. See Sumantra Ghoshal and Heike Bruch, "Beyond Motivation to Volition: Unleashing the Power of the Human Will," *Sloan Management Review* 44 (spring 2003).

5. See Hugo M. Kehr, *Souveränes Selbstmanagement* (Sovereign Self-Management) (Weinheim, Germany: Beltz, 2002).

6. See Hugo M. Kehr. "Integrating Motives, Goals, and Abilities: The Compensatory Model of Work Motivation and Volition," *Academy of Management Review* (forthcoming).

7. These strategies reflect the two core tasks of volition—creating energy for goal pursuit and suppressing emotions that impede goal pursuit. See Julius Kuhl and Arno Fuhrmann, "Decomposing Self-Regulation and Self-Control: The Volitional Components Inventory," in *Motivation and Self-Regulation Across the Life Span*, eds. J. Heckhausen and C. S. Dweck, (Cambridge, England: Cambridge University Press, 1998), 15–49.

8. Both strategies are a form of self-control that manipulates or suppresses emotions in favor of rational goals rather than productively combining

emotions with rationality as self-regulation does. See Julius Kuhl, "A Theory of Self-Regulation: Action Versus State Orientation, Self-Discrimination, and Some Applications," *Applied Psychology* 41 (1992): 97–129.

9. Csikszentmihalyi introduced the construct of *flow*, which describes a state of optimal or autotelic experience, implying maximum energy and total involvement in an activity that requires complete concentration. See Mihaly Csikszentmihalyi, *Flow: The Psychology of Optimal Experience* (New York: Harper & Row, 1990); Mihaly Csikszentmihalyi, "If We Are So Rich, Why Aren't We Happy?" *American Psychologist* 54 (1999): 821–827; and Mihaly Csikszentmihalyi and Judith LeFevre, "Optimal Experience in Work and Leisure," *Journal of Personality and Social Psychology* 56 (1989): 815–822.

10. See Kehr, *Souveränes Selbstmanagement.*

11. Volition theory addressed the phenomenon of increased energy in the face of setbacks with the "principle of difficulty." That principle states that effort for achieving a certain intention is a positive function of the perceived difficulty of implementing the intended action that obstacles lead to intensifying willpower. See Narziss Ach, *Über den Willensakt und das Temperament: Eine experimentelle Untersuchung* (On the Act of Will and Temperament: An Experimental Study) (Leipzig, Germany: Quelle & Meyer, 1910).

12. For volitional strategies of emotional self-regulation, see Julius Kuhl, "Action Control: The Maintenance of Motivational States," in *Motivation, Intention, and Volition*, eds. F. Halish and J. Kuhl (Berlin and Heidelberg, Germany: Springer, 1987), 279–291; and Julius Kuhl and Miguel Kazén, "Volitional Facilitation of Difficult Intentions: Joint Activation of Intention Memory and Positive Affect Removes Stroop Interference," *Journal of Experimental Psychology* 128 (1999): 382–399; and Ralf Erber and Maureen Wang Erber, "The Self-Regulation of Moods: Second Thoughts on the Importance of Happiness in Everyday Life," *Psychological Inquiry* 11 (2000): 142–148; and William N. Morris and Nora P. Reilly, "Toward the Self-Regulation of Mood: Theory and Research," *Motivation and Emotion* 11 (1987): 215–249.

13. See Julius Kuhl and Arno Fuhrmann, "Decomposing Self-Regulation and Self-Control: The Volitional Components Inventory," in *Motivation and Self-Regulation Across the Life Span*, eds. J. Heckhausen and C. S. Dweck, (Cambridge, England: Cambridge University Press, 1998), 15–49.

14. Ibid., and Kehr, *Souveränes Selbstmanagement.*

15. See Csikszentmihalyi, *Flow.*

16. See Kehr, *Souveränes Selbstmanagement.*

17. Consciously and deliberately considering emotions in decision processes is to be distinguished from emotional or purely emotion-driven decisions. Actively using one's emotions lies at the heart of emotional intelligence. See Peter Salovey and John D. Mayer, "Emotional Intelligence," *Imagination, Cognition, and Personality* 9 (1990): 185–211.

CHAPTER 6

1. Rosemary Stewart suggested the framework of demands, constraints, and choices as a way to think about managerial jobs in her book *Managers and Their Jobs* (London: Macmillan, 1967). See also Rosemary Stewart, *Choices for the Manager* (London: Prentice Hall, 1982).

2. See Henry Mintzberg, "Managerial Work: Forty Years Later," in *Executive Behaviour*, ed. E. Carlson (Uppsala, Sweden: Acta Universitatis Upsatensis, 1991).

3. Studies on the nature of managerial work are helpful for pointing out the risk of nonaction in managerial jobs, yet most of them provide evidence that, even in cases of similar jobs, managers differ noticeably in their extent of action-taking. See John Kotter, *The General Managers* (New York: The Free Press, 1982).

4. Stewart, *Choices for the Manager*.

5. See Colin P. Hales, "What Do Managers Do? A Critical Review of the Evidence," *Journal of Management Studies* 23 (1986): 88–115; Lance B. Kurke and Howard E. Aldrich, "Mintzberg Was Right! A Replication and Extension of the 'Nature of Managerial Work,'" *Management Science* 29 (1983): 975–984.

6. See Stewart, *Choices for the Manager*.

7. See Kotter, *The General Managers*. The importance of continuously clarifying and deepening one's personal agenda has also been highlighted by Peter Senge, *The Fifth Discipline: The Art & Practice of the Learning Organization* (New York: Doubleday, 1990).

8. The effects of concrete mental pictures of one's aims and the ways to achieve them have been described by Albert Bandura, "Human Agency in Social Cognitive Theory," *American Psychologist* 9 (1989): 1175–1184. He speaks of foresight that he considers a self-regulatory strategy that includes anticipating probable consequences of prospective actions as well as planning courses of action likely to produce desired outcomes. "Being converted into representations cognitively in the present, conceived future events are converted into motivators and regulators of behavior" (1179).

9. See Stewart, *Managers and Their Jobs*.

10. Typical managerial problems in goal pursuit are getting started,

being too easily distracted, giving up in the face of obstacles when increased effort and persistence are needed, or resuming action after disruptions. See Peter M. Gollwitzer, "The Volitional Benefits of Planning," in *The Psychology of Action*, eds. P. M. Gollwitzer and J. A. Bargh (New York: The Guilford Press, 1996), 287–312. Getting started with or resuming an interrupted goal pursuit is rather simple when the necessary actions are well practiced or routine. See J. A. Oullette and W. Wood, "Habit and Intention in Everyday Life: The Multiple Processes by Which Past Behavior Predicts Future Behavior," *Psychological Bulletin* 124 (1998): 54–74. Often, however, managerial behaviors are not routine. Consequently, persistence, discipline, and overcoming a disinclination to exhibit a certain behavior become critical to managerial action. See Veronika Brandstätter, Angelika Lengfelder, and Peter M. Gollwitzer, "Implementation Intentions and Efficient Action Initiation," *Journal of Personality and Social Psychology* 81 (2001): 946–960.

11. See F. Luthans and J. K. Larsen, "How Managers Really Communicate," *Human Relations* 39 (1986): 161–178; and R. Whitley, "On the Nature of Managerial Tasks and Skills: Their Distinguishing Characteristics and Organization," *Journal of Management Studies* 26 (1989): 209–224.

12. See Stewart, *Choices for the Manager*.

13. See Kotter, *The General Managers*.

14. See Stewart, *Choices for the Manager*.

15. See "Lufthansa 2000: Maintaining the Change Momentum," case study prepared by Heike Bruch and Sumantra Ghoshal (London: London Business School, 2000).

16. See Heike Bruch and Thomas Sattelberger, "Lufthansa's Transformation Marathon—A Process of Liberating & Focusing Change Energy," *Human Resources Management* 40 (2001): 249–259.

17. See Stewart, *Choices for the Manager*.

18. Several scholars have pointed out that in cases of crisis, failure, or urgency, managers tend to display irrational behaviors, such as the use of behavioral templates, reactiveness, displacement activities, or more extensive trial and error. See, for example, Irving L. Janis and Leon Mann, *Decision Making: A Psychological Analysis of Conflict, Choice, and Commitment* (New York: The Free Press, 1977). Managers try to cope with a problem by using the behavioral plans they already have rather than taking time for analyzing, developing, and choosing a satisfactory way out of a precarious situation. For a review on forms of nonaction, see Heike Bruch, *Leaders' Action: Model Development and Testing* (Munich: Hampp, 2003).

19. In his early work in 1985, Pinchot introduced mottoes as one of the guiding commands for intrapreneurs. See Gifford Pinchot, *Intrapreneuring:*

Why You Don't Have to Leave the Corporation to Become an Entrepreneur (New York: Harper & Row, 1985).

20. See Jennifer A. Chatman, Jeffrey T. Polzer, Sigal G. Barsade, and Margaret A. Neale, "Being Different Yet Feeling Similar: The Influence of Demographic Composition and Organizational Culture on Work Processes and Outcomes," *Administrative Science Quarterly* 43 (December 1998): 749–780.

21. For a discussion of culture, see Edgar Schein, *Organizational Culture and Leadership*, 2d ed. (San Francisco: Jossey-Bass, 1992).

22. Managerial tasks are discretionary and—what is important for action—involve choices, rather than being routinely executed or determined by external factors. Management can, therefore, be distinguished from administration by its ability to select and change. See Richard Whitley, "On the Nature of Managerial Tasks and Skills: Their Distinguishing Characteristics and Organization," *Journal of Management Studies* 26 (1989): 209–224. Findings of several studies indicate that managerial work is sufficiently loosely defined—i.e., nonprogrammed and hardly formalized or standardized—to be highly negotiable and susceptible to choice of both what is to be done and how it is to be done. See, for example, Colin P. Hales, "What Do Managers Do? A Critical Review of the Evidence," *Journal of Management Studies* 23 (1986): 88–115; and Henry Mintzberg, *The Nature of Managerial Work* (New York: HarperCollins Publishers, 1973). Although the scopes of higher hierarchical levels are broader than those of lower positions, managerial work involves a number of common choices regarding content and process. See Rosemary Stewart, *Contrasts in Management* (Maidenhead, England: McGraw-Hill, 1976).

23. See Denise M. Rousseau and Snehal A. Tijoriwala, "Assessing Psychological Contracts: Issues, Alternatives and Measures," *Journal of Organizational Behavior* 19 (1998): 679–695.

24. See "Hilti 2003: Maintaining a Proactive Sense of Urgency," case study prepared by Heike Bruch and Sabine Bieri (St. Gallen, Switzerland: University of St. Gallen, 2003).

25. See Harry Binswanger, "Volition and Cognitive Self-Regulation," *Organizational Behavior and Human Decision Processes* 50 (1991): 154–178.

26. See Stewart, *Choices for the Manager.*

27. Investigating the tactics used by people at work to influence their superiors, coworkers, and subordinates, Kipnis and colleagues found reason to be the most effective one. See David Kipnis and Stuart M. Schmidt, "Upward-Influence Styles: Relationship With Performance Eval,"

Administrative Science Quarterly 33 (1988): 528–542; and David Kipnis, Stuart M. Schmidt, and Ian Wilkinson, "Intraorganizational Influence Tactics: Explorations in Getting One's Way," *Journal of Applied Psychology* 65 (1980): 440–452.

28. See Michael Frese et al., "Personal Initiative at Work: Differences Between East and West Germany," *Academy of Management Journal* 39 (1996): 37–63.

29. This particular competence has been called *organizational awareness* and refers to an individual's ability to understand an organization's informal and formal structures, unspoken organizational constraints, underlying problems, opportunities, or political forces. See Lyle M. Spencer and Signe M. Spencer, *Competence at Work* (London: Hay McBer Research Press, 1994).

30. The belief in one's ability to accomplish certain tasks or to meet certain situational demands has been called *self-efficacy*. See Albert Bandura, *Self-Efficacy: The Expertise of Control* (New York: Freeman, 1997). There is sufficient empirical evidence indicating that people low in self-efficacy are unlikely to take action and that people high in self-efficacy are more likely to take action. See Jean M. Phillips and Stanley M. Gully, "Role of Goal Orientation, Ability, Need for Achievement, and Locus of Control in the Self-Efficacy and Goal-Setting Process," *Journal of Applied Psychology* 82 (1997): 792–802.

31. See Michael Frese et al., "Personal Initiative."

32. Vagueness of choices can lead to a subjective lack of control that—particularly in combination with high complexity, frequent interruptions, and being overburdened—is one of the central reasons of negative stress and learned helplessness. See Michael Frese, "Theoretical Models of Control and Health," in *Job Control and Worker Health*, eds. S. L. Sauter, J. J. Hurrel, and C. L. Cooper, (Chichester, England: Wiley, 1989): 107–108.

33. See Joseph A. Schumpeter, *Theorie der wirtschaftlichen Entwicklung* (Theory of Economic Development) (Leipzig, Germany: Duncker & Humblot, 1912), 110.

CHAPTER 7

1. See Robert G. Eccles and Nitin Nohria, *Beyond the Hype* (Boston: Harvard Business School Press, 1992).

2. See Icek Ajzen, *Attitudes, Personality, and Behavior* (Milton Keynes, CA: Open University Press, 1988); and Edward L. Deci and Richard M. Ryan, "The Support of Autonomy and the Control of Behavior," *Journal of Personality and Social Psychology* 53 (1988): 1024–1037.

3. See "The Transformation of BP: From a Divided Past to a Shared Future," case study prepared by Michelle Rogan, Lynda Gratton, and Sumantra Ghoshal (London: London Business School, 2001).

4. Social support facilitates coping with job requirements in two different ways. First, problem-focused coping is supported by instrumental and informative support such as advice, guidance, or backing. Second, emotion-focused coping is supported by informative and emotional support, which directly facilitates a person's ability to deal with his or her emotions. See James B. House, *Work, Stress and Social Support* (Reading, MA: Addison-Wesley, 1981).

5. See Richard S. Lazarus and Susan Folkman, *Stress, Appraisal and Coping* (New York: Springer, 1984).

6. We have found transformational leadership, as Bass and colleagues suggest, particularly supportive for purposeful action. See Bernard M. Bass and Bruce J. Avolio, *Improving Organizational Leadership Through Transformational Leadership* (Thousand Oaks, CA: Sage, 1994).

7. See Amy Wrzesniewski and Jane E. Dutton, "Crafting a Job: Revisioning Employees As Active Crafters of Their Work," *The Academy of Management Review* 26 (2001): 179–201.

8. See "Hilti 2003: Maintaining a Proactive Sense of Urgency," case study prepared by Heike Bruch and Sabine Bieri (St. Gallen, Switzerland: University of St. Gallen, 2003).

9. Few managers perceive and exploit their choices. See Rosemary Stewart, *Choices for the Manager* (London: Prentice Hall, 1982).

10. See Michael Frese et al., "Personal Initiative at Work: Differences Between East and West Germany," *Academy of Management Journal* 39 (1996): 37–63.

11. See Julius Kuhl and Miguel Kazén, "Volitional Facilitation of Difficult Intentions: Joint Activation of Intention Memory and Positive Affect Removes Stroop Interference," *Journal of Experimental Psychology* 128 (1999): 382–399.

12. See "Hilti 2003: Maintaining a Proactive Sense of Urgency."

CHAPTER 8

1. Organizational energy entails force, vitality, and endurance. It manifests as the proportion of temperament, intensity, tempo, and stamina of a company's change and innovation processes. See Amir Levy and Uri Merry, *Organizational Transformation* (New York: Praeger, 1986). The strength of organizational energy is reflected in a company's ability to activate its energy potential in the pursuit of its goals. See also Heike Bruch and Sumantra

Ghoshal, "Unleashing Organizational Energy," *Sloan Management Review*, 45 (fall 2003).

2. See Michael Tushman and Charles A. O'Reilly III, "Ambidextrous Organization: Managing Evolutionary and Revolutionary Change," *California Management Review* 38 (1996): 8–30.

3. James W. Dean Jr., Pamela Brandes, and Ravi Dharwadkar have described the causes and consequences of this energy state in their article "Organizational Cynicism," *Academy of Management Review* 23 (1998): 341–352.

4. For both a review and an important contribution, see Quy Nguyen Huy, "Emotional Balancing of Organizational Continuity and Radical Change: The Contribution of Middle Managers," *Administrative Science Quarterly* 47 (2002): 31–69.

5. The term *comfort zone* was introduced by John P. Kotter, "Leading Change: Why Transformation Efforts Fail," *Harvard Business Review* (March–April) 1995): 59–67.

6. Donald N. Sull, "Why Good Companies Go Bad," *Harvard Business Review* (July–August 1999).

7. Different reasons, such as emotional contagion, feeling affect vicariously, and behavioral imitation, can contribute to downward emotional spirals. See Janice R. Kelly and Segal Barsade, "Emotions in Small Groups and Work Teams," *Organizational Behavior and Human Decision Processes* 86 (2001): 99–130. The dynamic of collective emotion derives from imitating and exaggerating others' emotions. See Brian Parkinson, "Emotions Are Social," *British Journal of Psychology* 87 (1996): 663–684. For a review see Donald C. Hambrick and Richard A. D'Aveni, "Large Corporate Failures As Downward Spirals," *Administrative Science Quarterly* 33 (1988): 1–22.

8. For a discussion on the link between energy and performance, see Rob Cross, Wayne Baker, and Andrew Parker, "What Creates Energy in Organizations?" *Sloan Management Review* 44 (July 2003).

9. The term *acceleration trap* was introduced by Robert J. Zaugg and Norbert Thom, "Excellence Through Implicit Competencies: Human Resource Management—Organizational Development—Knowledge Creation," *Journal of Change Management* 3, no. 3 (2003): 1–21.

10. The term *organizational burnout* was introduced by James W. Greenwood III and James W. Greenwood, Jr., *Managing Executive Stress* (New York: Wiley, 1979).

11. For the strains of change, see Andrew Pettigrew and Richard Whipp, *Managing Change for Competitive Success* (Oxford and Cambridge, England: Blackwell, 1991).

12. See Thomas C. Davenport and John C. Beck, "Getting the Attention You Need," *Harvard Business Review* (September–October 2000).

13. Sometimes a profound trauma must take place in a company before it becomes aware of a threat and willing to change. This idea goes back to the process model of unfreezing-move-refreezing that Kurt Lewin introduced in his paper "Frontiers in Group Dynamics," *Human Relations* 1 (1947): 5–41. For a more recent description of that approach, see Michael Tushman and Charles A. O'Reilly III, "Ambidextrous Organization: Managing Evolutionary and Revolutionary Change," *California Management Review* 38 (1996): 8–30.

14. See "Lufthansa 2003: Energising a Decade of Change," case study prepared by Heike Bruch (St. Gallen, Switzerland: University of St. Gallen, 2003).

15. See Boas Shamir, Robert J. House, and Michael B. Arthur, "The Motivational Effects of Charismatic Leadership: A Self-Concept-Based Theory," *Organizational Science* 4 (1993): 577–594; and Peter M. Senge, *The Fifth Discipline: The Art & Practice of the Learning Organization* (New York: Doubleday, 1990).

16. VAIO stands for "Video Audio Integrated Operations," representing the challenge of integrating all of Sony's different product and service offerings. At the same time, it also symbolizes the need for combining analog (the wave of VA) and digital (IO) technologies. See "Sony: Regeneration (A and B)," cases prepared by Tomohiro Kida and Hidehiko Yamaguchi under the supervision of Sumantra Ghoshal (London: London Business School, 2002).

17. This is the model of leadership recommended by both W. Bennis, "Leadership of Change," and K. Weick, "Emergent Change as a Universal in Organizations," in *Breaking the Code of Change*, eds. M. Beer and N. Nohria (Boston: Harvard Business School Press, 2000), 113–122; 223–242.

18. See "Cartier: A Legend of Luxury," case study prepared by Sumantra Ghoshal, Francois-Xavier Huard, and Charlotte Butler (Fontainebleau, France: INSEAD-CEDEP, 1992).

CHAPTER 9

1. J. Kuhl, "Volitional Mediators of Cognition Behaviour Consistency: Self-Regulatory Processes and Action Versus State Orientation," in *Action Control: From Cognition to Behaviour*, eds. J. Kuhl and J. Beckmann (Berlin: Springer, 1985), 101–128.

2. Making the process of committing more difficult is effective because volition emerges only with difficulties. Easy or routine tasks do not need or

stimulate willpower. See Julius Kuhl and Miguel Kazén, "Volitional Facilitation of Difficult Intentions: Joint Activation of Intention Memory and Positive Affect Removes Stroop Interference," *Journal of Experimental Psychology* 128 (1999): 382–399.

3. A central finding of Ach's experiments was the "principle of specific determination," which states that the speed and likelihood of the enactment of an intention are positive functions of its specificity. See Narziss Ach, *Analyse des Willens* (Analysis of the Will) (Berlin: Urban & Schwarzenberg, 1935).

4. See "Lufthansa 2003: Energising a Decade of Change," case study prepared by Heike Bruch (St. Gallen, Switzerland: University of St. Gallen, 2003).

5. For the distinction of organizational and goal commitment, see T. E. Becker, "Foci and Bases of Commitment: Are the Distinctions Worth Making?" *Academy of Management Journal* 35 (1992): 232–244.

APPENDIX

1. We have written up these findings in an academic paper. See Heike Bruch, *Leaders' Action: Model Development and Testing* (Munich: Hampp, 2003).

2. See Heike Bruch and Sumantra Ghoshal, "Managerial Action: Construct Definition, Model Development and Testing," working paper, University of St. Gallen, St. Gallen, Switzerland, 2003. When this book went to press, the paper was under review by a scholarly journal. Any reader interested in this paper can obtain a copy by contacting either author.

Heike Bruch is professor and director at the Institute for Leadership and Human Resources Management at the University of St. Gallen (Switzerland). She is also research director of the Organizational Energy Consortium and academic director of the university's International Study Program.

Between 1999 and 2001 she was visiting scholar and senior research fellow at London Business School. During 1996 to 1999 she was research director and assistant professor of the Institute for Leadership and Human Resources Management at the University of St. Gallen and, from 1991 to 1996, lecturer at the University of Hanover (Germany). She earned her Ph.D. in business administration at the University of Hanover (1996) and her master's (1991) and bachelor's (1989) degrees in business administration at the Free University of Berlin.

Bruch's research is strongly focused on leadership. She works in close cooperation with international universities both in research and teaching. The focal points of her more recent research work are managers' emotions, volition, action, and leadership in change processes and organizational energy. She has written four books, edited six, and published more than forty articles in journals and books.

Sumantra Ghoshal is a fellow of the Advanced Institute of Management Research (United Kingdom) and a professor of strategy and international management at London Business School. He is a member of the Committee of Overseers of Harvard Business School and has served as the founding dean of the Indian School of Business.

With doctoral degrees from both MIT Sloan School of Management and Harvard Business School, Ghoshal serves on several corporate boards and has been nominated to the fellowships of the Academy of Management, the Academy of International Business, and the World Economic Forum.

He is the author of several books, including *Managing Across Borders: The Transnational Solution* and *The Individualized Corporation*, both coauthored with Christopher A. Bartlett. He has published more than seventy articles, ten of which appeared in the *Harvard Business Review*, and has received several awards, including the George Terry Book Award and the Igor Ansoff Award.